Steelhead Savvy

Tight Lines!
Jim Bedford

Jim Bedford

Frank
Amato
PORTLAND

Acknowledgments

The author extends his sincere appreciation to Frank and Nick Amato for their guidance and encouragement in putting this volume together as well as giving me the chance to write for *Salmon Trout Steelheader* on a regular basis. Special thanks go to my fishing partners and angling class students for their patience and indulgence relative to my incessant need for photographs and for the knowledge gained from their steelheading experiences that they shared. And, much gratitude is due my fishing widow of many years, Kathel, who has always understood my need to be standing in a steelhead or trout stream several days a week.

On the Cover: *Mike Cole with a nice steelhead on the Sustut River in British Columbia.*

Published in 1994 by Frank Amato Publications, Inc.
P.O. Box 82112, Portland, Oregon 97282
(503) 653-8108
ISBN: 1-878175-94-7
UPC: 0-66066-00199-3
Book Design: Charlie Clifford
Printed in U.S.A.
1 3 5 7 9 10 8 6 4 2

Contents

Introduction

Sparkling swift rivers, cedar lined bends, towering high banks, soaring eagles, water ouzel antics, stair step rapids, snow capped mountains . . . there is no doubt that the steelhead's fresh-water environment is beautiful and enchanting. The lure of what's around the next bend mesmerizes the angler as he or she wades or drifts a stream in search of its silver treasures. While the aesthetics of river steelheading are great the real icing on the cake is hooking up with the king of the river, the magnificent steelhead.

The goal of this volume is to help both the beginning and experienced river angler catch (and release) more steelhead. Considerable basic information will be shared but we will concentrate on the more subtle, advanced special techniques that will improve your success. I have tried to sort out some of the myths and fallacies that have been perpetuated about steelhead and provide you with lots of good, solid, scientifically based information. It is my hope that everyone who reads *Steelhead Savvy* will learn something new about steelhead and fishing for these great game fish.

1

What Makes a Steelhead Tick

If you are reading this book you probably already know a lot about the steelhead and are very fond of this special fish. Biology and life history can be a bit boring but the more we know about steelies the better we will be able to seek them out and get connected via rod and reel. Much has been learned and written about this species through scientific research. In this chapter I will attempt to interweave some of this scientific information with my, and my frequent fishing partners', experiences with these fish. I have pursued the mighty steelhead with great fervor for almost 30 years in Michigan, Indiana, Oregon, British Columbia and Alaska.

The Species

Steelhead are rainbow trout just like the Kamloops, red band and the farm raised variety you order in the restaurant. Even though these rainbows are the same species they obviously live in different habitats and behave differently. Steelhead is the term used for anadromous rainbow trout which Webster defines as rainbows that migrate up rivers from the sea to spawn in freshwater. As these fish have been introduced into many other waters of the world, self sustaining populations of steelhead have developed that remain in freshwater throughout their lives. Instead of migrating from the ocean to their natal streams they utilize large lakes such as the Great Lakes.

Some traditionalists from the Pacific Northwest still don't acknowledge that anadromous rainbows in the Great Lakes or other large inland lakes should be called steelhead. But rather than argue this point let's get on with learning more about this great fish no matter where it lives.

Early Stream or Hatchery Life

Virtually all steelhead spawn in mid to late winter or spring. There have been some fall spawning hatchery strains released into the Great Lakes but fall spawners are relatively rare. In most fairly fertile streams the young future steelhead or parr will spend two years growing to smolting size. In some special cases of perfect conditions the parr may reach smolting size in one year. More often the natal streams may be poor in nutrients and the young rainbows may require three or more years of stream life. A good number of Lake Superior tributaries and northern Pacific coastal rivers fall in this category.

In the hatchery the river part of the young steelhead's life is shortened to one year via constant, plentiful food and usually warmer water temperatures in the winter. Thus when you are trying to interpret hatchery plants and the return of the adults you can consider that the year planted was also the year that the fish smolted. The exception to this is when the hatchery fish are planted as fall fingerlings. These fish will have to spend one and a half years in the stream before smolting thus you have to add two calendar years to the planting year to know when to expect the adults to return. It should also be noted that the fall fingerlings normally do not survive very well unless planted in a special situation such as a chemically reclaimed marginal trout stream where the returns can be phenomenal.

As the parr begin the smolting process in late spring they become quite silvery. At this time they are also becoming imprinted to their natal stream so they will know where to return after a rapid growth period in the ocean or large lake. It is believed that they are imprinted to the area they resided as well as the whole river. In some systems the smolts must become imprinted to a series of rivers in order to be able to home on the stream that they were born and raised in. In general the strongest imprint is to the last river before they hit the ocean. For example almost all of the Deschutes steelhead will come back to the Columbia but there may be some straying into other tributaries of the big river before they reach the natal stream.

The imprinting time period is relatively short so if hatchery fish are not planted at the right time there could be considerable straying away from the planting site. Overall, however steelhead in both the Pacific and the Great Lakes zero in on their natal or planted stream with consistent regularity.

Lynda Hayslette about to release a Rogue River (Michigan) hen.

To the Big Water and Back

Steelhead will spend from one to five years in the ocean or lake before returning to the tributaries. Some will migrate to spawn more than once while others will save it all up for one trip. Those that return after one year are known as "half pounders" on the west coast and "skippers" in the midwest. They will weigh from one to three pounds some will be sexually immature while others will be precocious males. Some rivers have a preponderance of these fish such as Oregon's Rogue. In the Great Lakes we seem to have more of them when growing conditions were especially good in both the river and the lake. If the smolts left the river at a large average size look for lots of skippers in those rivers the following fall.

The majority of the steelhead make their first journey back to freshwater after two or three years. In general, especially on the West Coast, the majority of the hatchery fish will be two salt steelhead while the wild fish will tend to wait until they are larger three salt fish. We don't see much difference in Michigan between wild and hatchery fish, probably since all of the hatchery fish have wild parents.

Some steelhead will not return until they have fed at sea for four years and in a few rare cases five years. These will be your trophy fish as they have concentrated on eating and not procreation. Most of the four salt fish will have already spawned once and will not be much larger than they were on their first spawning run. This is because spawning takes a lot out of the fish and it takes some time just to recover the weight they lost on their trip up river.

Different Strains

Each river will have its own mix of return fish and past records will help you decide where to go if you're looking for that one trophy or are interested in doing battle with several two salt fish. Likewise the timing of the runs varies with each river system and studying the catch records will be an important part of planning your excursions.

Obviously a major consideration is whether you are dealing with summer or winter running strains. There are also runs that occur in the fall and in the spring. The spreading out of the return of steelhead has assured their survival in the case of weather or some other cataclysmic event that wipes out a whole run of fish.

Summer steelhead evolved because some habitats were unreachable because of barriers present during winter water conditions. Sometimes the barrier was ice in northern British Columbia and Alaska streams in the winter and if the fish waited until spring there was too much water from the spring floods and too little time to travel considerable distances to the spawning gravel. Summer runs have been successfully planted in streams where there is no reason for summer steelhead to evolve in order to provide a summer river fishery. Indiana's main motivation for planting the Skamania strain was not to provide a river fishery but mainly an attempt to keep the fish in southern Lake Michigan in the summer.

Wild, fall running steelhead are present in many Great Lakes tributaries with no obvious explanation. There is such a short run to the spawning riffles that these fish could easily make the trip in the spring. These fish are great fighters so I'm glad they run in the autumn even if we don't know why. Rainfall plays a big roll in how many come up the rivers in October and November so midwest anglers should keep a sharp eye on the weather and hope for periodic heavy rains. These fish have no urgency to reach the spawning areas so the lower reaches of the rivers are the places to intercept these steelies.

Winter weather usually shuts down the runs of steelhead in the Great Lakes while this is the time of the main runs on the West Coast. Freshets are again the key to bringing in the fish and if there has been a fairly lengthy dry spell you definitely want to be on your favorite river as the water drops after a big rain finally arrives. December and January seem to be the main months for hatchery runs while the wild fish will be spread out over the winter with a higher percentage arriving in February and March.

Spring is the time for the biggest numbers of fish to hit the rivers in the midwest. Peak runs depend on the severity of the winter and how soon warm spring days arrive. They usually occur in the last half of March through April but you don't want to time your fishing based on previous peak times because every year is different. Runs are also influenced by latitude with most Lake Superior runs not peaking until May, even with a warm spring.

Spring runs also occur in the West and usually they are underfished. Many anglers are now concentrating on spring Chinook or they just think of steelheading as a winter sport. Catch records don't always help because there are only a few anglers out fishing. Thus you may have to do a little detective work, but the rewards can be great.

River Migration

The rate at which steelhead travel upstream is dependent on many variables including the water temperature, height and turbidity, distance they have to travel and how close they are to spawning. If the rivers are low and cold look for the steelies to hang around tidewater or the big deep holes in the lower sections of the rivers. Conversely, if it is getting close to spawning time and the water has been up and relatively warm (40+) you should probably start your search for these silver treasures in the upper reaches of the stream. Learning and recording how steelhead react to weather and water conditions in different rivers at different times are keys to success. Finding the fish and making a good presentation are far more important to getting hooked up than any particular bait or lure.

Little Appetite

Research has shown that steelhead, especially winter runs, usu-

Ken Burda battles a Bulkley River steelhead.

ally do not actively feed on their river migrations. They do, however, remain opportunistic and will accept a bait that looks and smells right and is presented right to their nose. Then, because it tastes and feels good, the steelie will hold on to it long enough for you to set the hook. This helps explain why drifting real eggs, nymphs and shrimp is so productive. Even though the anadromous rainbows often eventually expel the food items they give anglers with a slow reaction time a chance.

Immature skippers are exceptions in that they frequently have the feed bag on and summer steelhead are also prone to occasionally searching out food items. Then there are the oddball fish that break all the rules. On a frigid winter day when the water temperature had been 32 degrees or less for several weeks one of my partners caught a rather robust looking hatchery steelhead. Upon cleaning the fish he discovered its stomach to be absolutely packed with small, dark insect nymphs. Who knows how or why that fish gathered up all those tidbits when biological activity in the river had to be at a standstill.

The travel lanes of the steelies, where they lie on their journey, where they are most likely to hit and how to pick these havens out will be discussed in the next chapter.

2

Haunts of the
Migrating **S**teelhead

I love rivers or maybe addicted is a better description of my attachment to moving water. It is for certain that I especially enjoy walking along and wading rivers eagerly anticipating what might be around the next bend. A large part of the attraction is in trying to find and catch steelhead as they traverse their natal river back to the spawning grounds.

A major reason river fishing is so appealing to me is that you are able figure out where the steelies will be using your own senses. You don't need a fish locator, depth finder, pH meter, dissolved oxygen probe or other electronic gadget to tell you where to cast your offering. Sight is of course your most important sense when unlocking a river's secrets but other senses come into play as well.

Your sense of touch will be used a lot as you fish for the mighty steelhead. The periodic tick on the bottom will tell you that your rig is near where the fish are lurking. And, when the pull on your lure is just right you know you're in a flow that you have learned is to the steelhead's liking.

I have a fishing buddy who claims to be able to smell steelhead in the river. At first this may be pretty hard to believe but then I thought about the peculiar odor many steelies exude when you land them. Well, I think I just might have detected that odor on the stream a time or two myself.

Probably it was more related to the water "looking" just perfect for a resting steelhead. There will be times when experience and intuition are relied upon when searching for anadromous rainbows but vision remains the key sense when decoding the river for the locations of its silver visitors. And it is probably past visual experiences that lead to your thinking that a spot may hold fish even if you can't see the cover. Of course, knowing something about the biology and habits of steelhead is also important in finding and getting hooked up to these treasures of our rivers.

Cover is Key

Overhead cover seems to be especially important to migrating steelhead. They have just left the depths of a large lake, ocean or bay so it is easy to relate to how they might feel vulnerable in their new, much shallower surroundings. Overhanging trees, logs, stumps, root wads and large boulders are examples of favored cover. Cover is also provided by water depth and turbidity or a choppy surface.

The steelies are on the move and tend to align themselves with the main current. As the trout migrate upstream they will need to find resting places in or near the main flow of the river. Thus when you find obstacles in the major currents that both block the water and offer overhead protection you have located a prime holding spot for migrating steelhead.

An angler battles a steelhead hooked near a log.

Resting Spots

When these fish have traveled through long, shallow rapids they will look for the first resting spot they can find. This is usually in the tailout of the next deep pool or run. Any bedrock or clay ledges, logs or boulders in this area should be fished very hard when steelhead are on the move.

The body or deepest part of the pool will hold resting steelies but usually it is tougher to get them to respond to your offering in this location. However, when the water is very cold and low steelhead will be concentrated in the deep water and more time should be spent fishing for them there.

The upper or head ends of pools deserve lots of attention. It is here that the steelhead lay just before they attempt to move through the next shallow stretch of water. These fish are anxious to move on and are frequently very aggressive. The broken surface from the upstream riffle or rapids provides protection so that these steelies may lay right at the lip of the gravel bar.

Steelhead will also be concentrated in slots because of their desire to be in or near fast current yet not have to fight it. Slots are created in areas where the main flow intersects the back eddies that are caused by the movement of water along an irregular bank or one with lots of brush, fallen trees or other cover. These narrow, quiet water areas are perfect resting locations for steelies and you should make lots of presentations to them.

Riffles would seem to be an illogical place to find resting steelhead because they are rarely deeper than a few feet. As it turns out they are probably the most dependable place to find summer run steelhead. Frequently it has been written that steelies are attracted to riffles because there is more oxygen there. This is almost never the case as the dissolved oxygen is at saturation throughout the stream in most of our steelhead rivers. The only exception might be when you have an enriched river with a long slow stretch of water. Here you might find dissolved oxygen at a supersaturation level in the late afternoon and a bit below saturation in the early morning.

The real attraction is the choppy surface which keeps the steelies hidden. Riffles are the food factories of the river and since summer runs occasionally may feed this could be another reason for them frequently holding here. Since the riffles were "home" to the steelhead during their first years of life there may also be some kind of instinctive "memory" attraction. Regardless of the reason, if the riffle is deep enough and the surface is well chopped up so that you can't see the bottom clearly, fish it hard.

Not Just Behind

Big rocks or boulders form prime places for steelhead to rest as they can block strong current and provide cover. It is important to realize that the boulder slows the flow in front of it as well as providing slack water behind it. Usually you have a better chance to catch a steelie in front of the rock as this location is easier to fish. In addition the steelhead in this lie are perhaps more aggressive, at least they have been for me.

On many steelhead streams you encounter long stretches of flat water with little or no cover. You should bypass this water quickly and then fish the first good holding water at the upper end of the flat water very hard. Steelhead will be concentrated here.

New Water

The frequent mixing of the water in a steelhead river keeps water conditions such as turbidity and temperature constant. However when a tributary joins the river or a large spring flows in you will find an area of different water quality conditions that may attract steelies. The extent that this new water will stay separated and different depends on the size of the influent stream and the rate of mixing. Usually the mixing will be complete in a riffle or two but if the tributary enters on the outside of a long slow bend the water may remain separate for a long time. For example in Michigan the Rogue River water stays fairly intact for several miles after it joins the Grand River, especially when both rivers are relatively low.

Often the tributary and always the spring will be warmer in the winter and cooler in the summer than the main stream. In both seasons steelhead are likely to prefer the temperature of the influent water so they will be attracted to it and more active there.

If the tributary is the natal or spawning stream for many of the steelhead in the river system or if it is heavily planted look for steelies to stack up in or near its influence on the main river prior to making a spawning run up it. Using Michigan's Rogue River as an example again we have the Grand's heaviest planted tributary and one that is almost always clearer than the bigger river. Thus we have multiple reasons to fish the edge of the Grand downstream from where the Rogue flows in.

Concentrate First

A basic tenet of steelheading is to learn a small amount of river well rather trying a different stretch or a different river each time you go. This rule applies especially to those drift fishing but is also a good idea for all methods of fishing. As you experience success it is important to file a description of the fish holding areas in your memory bank. Each steelhead you catch should help make it easier for you to hook your next one. By the same token cataloging the water that consistently fails to yield steelies will help you eliminate some casts and become more efficient on the river.

Then Branch Out

Once you have a number of steelies under your belt you can begin to disregard the rule of concentrating on a few reaches of river. You will be most proficient when fishing water that you are very familiar with but one of the great joys of steelheading is exploring new water. I really get fired up when I know I will be wading a brand new section and the word is out that fish are in the river. It is a challenge to test your water reading skills and very exhilarating to see something new around each bend. And then when you strike silver in that new run that looked so great. Wow!

Holding Water Subtleties

There will be times when you find fishy looking water that is hard to read and does not have any obvious slots or cover. In a situation like this you want to fish the water fairly fast looking for anything that might provide a little more protection. In several magazine articles I have described a very productive bend in Michigan's Pere Marquette River which illustrates this perfectly. The current and depth were ideal throughout the long bend but there weren't any logs or other bank cover. In one spot a small branch just touched the water and rippled the surface just a bit. Every steelhead I've caught in that bend was hooked right under or below that branch.

An additional clue as to where to cast in relatively non-descript water lies in the bubble or foam on the surface. The areas where fish are the most concentrated are also likely to be where the main flow is located. So, whenever you are at a loss on where to cast, fish under the bubbles.

Better Vision

A billed cap or visor and polarized sunglasses are essential parts of your river steelheading arsenal. The bill cuts the glare on the polaroids and the glasses cut the surface glare so you can spot underwater cover, current blockers and sometimes even fish. I usually carry two pair, one with a light amber tint which I wear most of the time, especially under low light conditions, and a pair with a dark gray tint for bright days. In addition to looking below the surface watch for bulges in the surface currents that indicate underwater logs and large rocks.

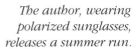

The author, wearing polarized sunglasses, releases a summer run.

In Conclusion

Always keep in mind that tributary rivers to the ocean or large lakes are highways for steelies on their spawning migration. The current is both the steelhead's guidance system and its obstacle. These fish always orient to the current but look for ways to avoid it when traveling and at rest. They also exhibit a strong need or desire for protective cover on their river travels. Thus the key things to look for are places where the main current is slowed or blocked and good overhead cover is present.

3

More Quality Time on the River

Even though I pull my waders on and venture into a stream more than 100 days each year my time on the water is very precious to me. Thus, much thought is given to the tackle and equipment needed for each outing. My goal is to have the right gear along with repair materials to keep me on the river effectively fishing and not walking back to the car for some forgotten item or to replace something that has broken.

In fact to help me remember everything before I leave home I go through a little rhyme...rod, reel; net, creel; waders, meal; vest and zeal. This aids in making sure the required gear gets into the car and to the access point. Then, the rhyme is repeated after donning the waders and vest before departing up the river.

The size and condition of the river you are planning to fish will affect your gear selection. Often you must wait until you arrive at the stream to decide which outfit to take. Thus your car or truck may have to take on the role of a mini tackle shop on trips where you're uncertain of river conditions.

Rod and Reel

Starting with the basics, the rod and reel, it is always a good idea to have an extra rod and reel along or several if you plan to use different techniques or fish dissimilar rivers. My rod cases are large enough to hold two rods and I pair up the same or similar rods in them so I always have a spare.

Not only does it make sense to bring a spare reel in the car but it is a good idea to carry one with you on the river. In addition to mechanical failures such as a broken bail spring the reel may be rendered inoperable by sand, ice or damage when dropped.

Line

Make sure you've got fresh line on your reel and that the spool is full. Remember that you don't need to change all the monofilament on the spool each time, just the top 50 yards of "working line". Use a blood knot to attach new line to your "backing". As you are fishing you'll be clipping off a foot or two of line that gets worn each time you change terminal rigs. When that blood knot starts to show on a long cast or you've spent several days on the river it's time to change the working line. Even the most expensive premium monofilament is a small part of your total angling costs but is a critical link to your success.

It also makes sense to carry extra reel spools filled with fresh line in your vest. Between the spool on the spare reel and the two in my vest I usually have an extra of the same pound test I am using along with one lighter and one heavier. That way I can switch to a different pound test if river conditions change or if I need to cast farther or horse steelhead out of the brush or some other reason. And if a steelhead does happen to do some major damage to my line on the rocks or a major tangle occurs I can replace the line with the same pound test.

One more important part of being prepared relative to your line is making sure your knots are secure. Moisten the knot and pull it tight very slowly. Always check it before you cast. Mono doesn't always slide together just right and the knot may end up being less than 50 percent of the line strength. Don't let a big steelhead discover this before you do and retie.

Spare Parts

Even though you are carrying a spare reel a small maintenance kit should be tucked away in your vest. Reel oil is very helpful in keeping your reel running smoothly and when using a cast and retrieve method a quiet, velvety-running reel is a big plus in detecting soft takes. Also, don't forget if your reel is squeaking there is metal to metal contact and unnecessary wear is occurring.

Because the bail spring is probably the most likely part to fail carrying an extra one (or pair for some models) is good insurance. If I break a bail spring I usually switch to my spare reel rather than changing it on the river. But, if something goes wrong with the spare you can still change on the stream which essentially gives you a double backup if you experience reel problems. A reel takedown tool which comes with many models or a small screwdriver and wrench should also be in a handy spot in your vest. It will be needed to replace a bail spring or if you need to tighten up a nut or screw or open up the reel to solve such dilemmas as a sand grain in the wrong place.

While I always carry a cased spare rod in a drift boat it is obviously not very handy to carry a spare rod when you're wading. You can carry some repair items that help keep you fishing if you should get unlucky and damage your rod. In a small reclosable plastic bag I have extra tip tops, single foot guides, ferrule cement, matches and a roll of black plastic electrical tape. If you damage the tip top you can replace it with the hot melt ferrule cement. Likewise you can replace a broken guide by taping a new one on in its place. If you break the rod near the tip you can keep fishing with a new tip top or if you don't have one with a large enough tube for the fracture point you can tape on a single foot guide.

If you break your rod somewhere in the middle you probably will have to head for the car and your spare rod. In a real pinch you can use tape to keep you fishing. One day I broke a graphite rod leaning on a feisty steelhead. After recovering from the shock of the loud "rifle crack" when it snapped, I even managed to land the steelie with the rod tip section slid down to the fish.

It was a considerable distance back to the car and there were a bunch of good runs to fish, so I overlapped the broken ends about three inches with the tip underneath and wrapped it with about half a roll of tape. The bandaged rod still cast quite well but I was concerned about setting the hook. The rod was pretty wobbly by the time I made it to the car but I landed two steelies with the splinted rod. Certainly a better deal than not being able to fish at all.

Nets

The net part of the rhyme may not apply to many western steelheaders but for me and my narrow, brushlined home rivers in Michigan with a paucity of gravel bars it is the preferred landing tool. There are also times, when wading wide shallow rivers, that it is a long way to shore. The net should be good sized so that you can corral the steelhead quickly and easily. Attach the net in such a way that keeps the net bag out of the brush. I generally carry it with an elastic cord around my shoulder and then use a heavy duty rubber band to gather and hold the net bag up around the base of the handle. Clipping it to the top of the back of your vest with a downrigger release is an even better idea. If you are not a net carrier perhaps this part of the rhyme will help you remember that tailing glove.

Fish in Tow

It is pretty evident that a big steelhead won't fit in a creel but the word rhymes and reminds me to make sure to bring a stringer along. While I rarely keep a steelhead if I do accidently gill hook one or decide to keep a hatchery fish a stringer is the handiest way to haul it. When your are wading a stringer allows you to trail the fish behind keeping you from having to pick it up, set it down on the bank and go back for it after you have fished through a run or bend. I prefer the stringer with nylon locking snaps because it is quiet and secure and by putting one snap in each jaw I end up with a convenient handle sling to carry the fish when walking the bank.

Tom Moore battles a steelhead with net ready.

Waders

Obviously just remembering your waders is an important part of being prepared for a day on the river. If you are a hard core, year-round river rat like me you may have more than one pair of different length, warmth or boot soles. Or, perhaps extra wading shoes with different soles or "add on" sandals with felts or cleats. If you have some of these options it is important to consider the river you're heading for and how slippery the rocks might be, how cold and or deep the water, etc.

When the weather is cold I always carry an extra pair of waders in the car along with a change of clothes so if I take a dive or tear a major hole in my boots I can retreat and start over. In my vest I also carry a wader patching kit which consists of hot melt flexible glue, matches or a lighter, Aquaseal and its accelerator Cotol. For quick temporary repairs I dab on the hot melt glue. A more dependable repair with the Aquaseal takes an hour or two but has the advantage of doing the job even if the waders are wet.

Nourishment

The meal part of the rhyme is simply a reminder not to forget your lunch. Additionally I like to pack snacks to nibble on when I am fishing. Fruit, candy, raw vegetables and nuts can all be tucked in a vest pocket in case you get hungry and the fish allow you time to eat.

Tackle Toter

We have already mentioned several things that should be carried in your vest to help keep you fishing and improve your success. The vest is the wading angler's tackle box and a critical part of your gear.

Terminal tackle is obviously the key item in a well stocked vest. The drift angler should have his or her sinkers, hooks, leader spools, swivels, yarn, drift lures and bait well organized. Lots of pre-tied rigs should be wrapped around leader cards ready to go. The hardware tossers and plug pullers should have their lures organized by size and finish. The selection of lures that you carry on the stream should be influenced by the size, water level and condition (water clarity, stain, etc.) of the river.

Other items to include in your vest that will help you be prepared and more effective are a line clipper, knife, scissors, hook hone or file, sunglasses, thermometer, pliers, penlight, scale, compass, gloves, plastic fish bag, attractant scent, aspirin, bandaids and disinfectant and a notebook and pencil. In the summertime you may want to make some ajustments such as taking out the gloves and adding insect repellent and sun screen.

Waterproof on Top

If rain is a possibility and it is cool or cold out I wear a raincoat because it is also a good windbreaker. Likewise if I am fishing deep water it comes in handy keeping my elbows dry. However, when it's balmy out packing a folded raincoat in the big pocket in the back of your vest keeps you from sweating when it is not raining and keeps you fishing if the heavens open up.

Recording the Memories

A pocket, point-and-shoot camera packed in your vest will greatly enhance each steelhead outing. Action shots and recording the beauty of the setting become possible when you have your camera along. And, being able to take photos of those steelies makes them much easier to release.

Wading Belt

With all of this gear you may think that your well stocked vest will weigh a ton. Well, mine weighs less than five pounds. But, even that is a lot of weight to carry on your shoulders all day. Here is where a wading belt can help. By wearing my vest inside my waders much of the weight of both the vest and the waders rides on my hips. Of course the wading belt also serves to slow the intake of water if you take a spill or a point of attachment for your wading staff cord.

Positive Attitude

Zeal is usually a given for most of us when we hit the river chasing the magnificent steelhead. However, sometimes a scant run of fish, bad weather, poor river conditions or too many other anglers dampen our spirits. So, along with all your other gear, be sure and pack an extra dose of confidence and zeal to help insure your success.

4

Setting the Table for the King

A n axiom of steelheading is that the angler who makes the most good presentations to prime holding water will be the most consistent in hooking these silver prizes. Accurate casting, reading holding water and gauging currents, selecting proper weight and picking the right lure type and color are all important components of a good presentation. Sometimes it is easy to make a good presentation while at other times it can be a tough puzzle.

Steelheading can be frustrating when you know steelies are present but can't seem to put a lure or bait that they will take in the right place. For example, I encountered a very narrow fast run cutting through the bedrock below a hatchery on a small creek. The surrounding water was quite shallow so I figured there had to be steelhead in the run.

With a spinner I had to cast straight upstream and then crank like crazy to keep it moving faster than the current and spinning. If there were steelhead resting in the notches of bedrock in the chute there was little chance they would see the spinner in time to intercept it.

Drifting a corkie and eggs combo through the fast run also failed to draw a response. Even though this offering was moving slightly slower than the spinner it was also less visible in the froth.

The answer was wading out directly above the boiling dark water and backing a plug down through. The current pulled violently on the wobbling lure and drove it to the bottom. Several times the pressure let up on the plug as it found some slack spots in the turbulence. When the plug got caught in the current again it almost felt like a fish.

However, there was no doubt when the plug entered another slack spot and was hammered by a steelhead. Luckily I had a good grip on the rod. After several jumps and a short trek downstream I was able to corral a red sided buck that had inhaled the plug and was solidly hooked with both trebles.

The two most important components of making consistent good presentations to steelies are knowing where they lay and making accurate casts. Time on the river is the best way to learn the habits of steelhead and how to read the water they are holding in. Hopefully the previous chapters on the fish and its habitat will shorten your learning time or help hone the river decoding skills you already have.

Casting to the Fish

For long casts in relatively open water you can't beat the level wind outfit. This reel gives you maximum control on the distance your offering travels because you can thumb the spool to slow it down or put the brakes on your lure or bait. Its free spool feature also aids in your presentation by allowing you to easily feed line and extend your drift.

However for shorter casts in tight situations I think that a high quality spinning reel is superior. The main reason is that it takes no effort to get the cast started. With the level wind you need to heave pretty hard to get the spool rotating. While it is a bit more difficult, with practice you can feather the line to slow your lure down if needed to make it land in the right spot. My favorite cast is the underhand pendulum cast. It is accomplished by letting about four feet of line hang off the rod tip and swinging the lure back. Then, with a snap of the wrist, swing the lure forward. This will line drive your offering to the target. If you are casting bait you want to tone down the forward snap of your wrist and lob your eggs or shrimp to the landing area.

The underhand cast is especially accurate because you can watch the lure during the whole process and easily make mid air corrections. Since the technique keeps your offering close to the water you can flip it under overhanging trees, rock ledges, logs and streamside brush. Most of my fishing is done in small to medium sized streams and even when there aren't overhead obstacles I stick with this cast because it is so accurate.

When you are trying to cast underneath low overhangs it is often helpful to get lower yourself. The kneepads on my waders get lots of use because I don't hesitate to kneel on the sand or gravel bar if it will help me deliver my lure to the target. Of course, if another steelheader happens by he will probably think that I've decided that the only way I'll ever catch a steelie is through prayer.

Judging the Currents

The drift angler not only has to cast accurately he or she also has to read the currents. For the most part the drifted offering is at the mercy of the current. Thus you have to make sure that your terminal rig lands in the right place upstream of the holding area so that it will follow a fish catching path. In addition to getting your offering in the right current lane you also need to use the correct amount of lead to get it near the bottom and have it land far enough upstream so that it is in the hitting zone as it drifts where you expect the fish to be.

Using a fluorescent main line will help you follow the course of your drift and may allow for some mid drift corrections. But, more importantly it will tell you the path of that particular drift with that cast and help you place your next cast to cover all of the holding water.

Long Distance Calls

On larger rivers making good presentations to steelhead often means casting long distance. Pick casting reels with larger spool diameters and then don't rely as much on the backlash control system. In spinning reels try models with longer spools which allow you to cast farther simply because there is less of a lip or line gap developing as the line coils off the spool. Spool diameter can also play an important role here as well as a more friction free spool lip.

Smaller line diameter will also add distance to your presentations. With monofilament you can either choose a lighter pound test or pick one of the new fine diameter premium lines. These special high tensile strength lines usually sacrifice some abrasion resistance so it is important to change them frequently.

You can get abrasion resistance with an even smaller diameter by using the new generation braided lines. In addition to letting you cast farther they make it easier to set the hook on those long dis-

Joe Burcar bows to a steelie hooked close to the opposite bank.

tance steelhead because of their lack of any significant stretch. One of the drawbacks to making good presentations with the braided lines is their high visibility. You can overcome this by using a leader but then you lose the advantage of their increased strength. And, the lack of stretch in the line may put extra stress on the leader. A better solution is to darken the last five or six feet of line with a permanent ink marker—some already on the market have been specially designed just for this purpose. Another possible drawback to these high tech braids is that they float. I've found that on sweep casts it is a little harder to get my lure down because there is a lot of buoyant line in the water.

Selecting heavier lures or adding weight to your drift rig will add casting distance but you must take care to not overdo it and adversely affect your presentation. More lead may slow your drift unnaturally and cause it to snag up and often heavier lures will have less action.

Special Techniques

As you fish a river there will continue to be situations like the fast chute described earlier which require special presentations. An example might be when you encounter an overhanging tree or bush with branches dragging in the water. Great cover but how do you get to the fish?

The diving plug can again come to the rescue. Quietly maneuver yourself into position above the tree. Cast and let the plug float down to the edge of the branches. Pull back hard against the current causing the plug to dive to the bottom. By easing up just a little you can get the current to carry the plug under the brush but not allow it to float back to the surface. Expect a hard strike as you have invaded a "safe haven" and then be ready to pressure the steelie out of trouble with your rod kept low to the water. You don't want to encourage the fish to roll or, heaven forbid, jump in this situation.

Another technique that works for getting underneath surface obstacles is back bouncing a bait or drift lure to the fish. In this case use extra weight and lift the sinker off the bottom by pulling back with the rod. This can even be done with a heavy spinner or spoon. Instead of lifting the sinker off the bottom and letting the current carry it back you lift the spinner up off the bottom by holding it against the current. The spinning resistance will cause the spinner to rise and you get it to move downstream by slacking off and feeding line so that it stops spinning and sinks back to the bottom.

While generally you are trying to drift your offering naturally with the current sometimes you can add to your chances by breaking this rule. When your bait or drift gets to the end of the drift, even if you have extended it by freespooling with your baitcasting reel, allow it to swing across the current until it is directly below you. Steelhead love a sweeping bait and won't be spooked by this unnatural drift like a stream wary trout might be.

Close First

Whether you are drifting or casting always remember to cover the holding water close to you first and then systematically work the run or hole further away. Also, try to get into a position so that you can work the holding water from downstream up. This will be least disruptive to the rest of the hole, especially if you hook a fish and can keep it from making a strong run upstream.

Look for more on getting your offering to these silver migrants in the methods chapters. Obviously presentations are intertwined with the techniques that you are using.

5

Drifting Along

Drift fishing is the most popular technique used to capture steelhead, especially the winter run variety. Frequently the question asked a successful steelheader is not what method he was using but whether it was eggs, sand shrimp or, in the Midwest, wigglers that did the trick.

The goal of the drift angler is to keep his or her offering drifting naturally with the current in water likely to hold resting steelhead. The basic rigging includes a leader and hook, dropper for a sinker and a mainline from the reel usually connected to a swivel.

Rigging Time

A three-way swivel is the focal point of most drift rigs used in the Midwest. The mainline is tied to one loop of the swivel, the sinker dropper line to another and the leader to the last ring. Most western anglers and a growing number of Great Lakes' steelheaders use two-way swivels because they are cheaper and save rigging time. Rather than having to tie on a dropper for your sinker simply leave a long tag end on your leader knot to the swivel and attach the weight to it.

Not tying one knot may not sound like much of a time saver but one of the biggest drawbacks to drift fishing is the rigging time. Losing your whole rig can mean four knots to tie plus baiting the hook and attaching a sinker. Without a doubt one of the most important things you can do to become a more successful drift angler is to reduce your down time.

A good example occurred on Michigan's Grand River at Sixth Street Dam where I was casting my usual weighted spinner while my partner was drifting eggs. The water was high and quite turbid and my buddy's slow moving, well scented milking spawn sack was definitely a superior technique for the conditions. But, the rocks were taking their toll and he was frequently breaking off. Three times I hooked steelies from the run we were sharing while he was retying. One bright henfish added insult to injury by dousing him with water on a towering leap right at his feet while he was engrossed in digging in his vest for more terminal gear. Throughout this discussion on drift fishing an overiding theme will be suggestions on increasing your time in the water on each outing.

Terminal Tackle

When selecting swivels pick the smallest size you can find that is still strong enough to hold a big steelie. Choosing high quality barrel or crane type swivels is a good idea but ball bearing ones are not necessary. Black or dull brass are the best finishes because you don't want the steelhead to be alarmed by it or strike it by mistake.

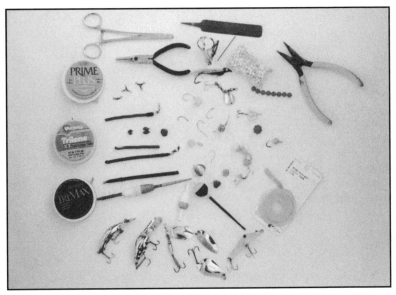

Terminal gear and the tools used to rig it.

A black permanent ink marker can be used to touch up swivels shined by banging on the rocks.

Since many of the runs and holes in Great Lakes tributaries are lined with sand or small gravel, split shot works well as sinkers and are very convenient. Just squeeze the right number or size onto your dropper and you're in business.

When larger rocks become the predominant substrate it is time to switch to lead of a uniform diameter so that it is less likely to hang up in crevices of the rocks. Hollow pencil lead is squeezed on your dropper just like split shot, vary the length rather than the number to get the right weight for the drift you are fishing.

Solid pencil lead can also be used and is usually attached using surgical tubing. The tubing is cinched over one eye of a three-way swivel or is attached to one loop of a two-way using a small snap that is pierced through the tubing. While pencil lead is less likely to get caught in the rocks than split shot it does hang up. When this happens, however, it will often just pull out of the tubing so you only have to slide a new piece in place to get back fishing.

In recent years an even more snag resistant sinker has become popular. The Slinky Drifter is a piece of hollow nylon cord that is filled with lead balls and then each end is melted shut with a hole or snap molded into one end for attachment. The nylon is very slippery and slides over the rocks and snags. Its only drawback is that the nylon adds water resisting bulk to the sinker so more weight must be used to get to the same depth and it is more difficult to get it down quickly when needed.

Near But Not On

The axioms that you need to present your offering right on the bottom for steelhead or if you are not hanging up on a regular basis you're not getting deep enough, are emphatically false. Steelhead orient to the stream bottom and frequently rest with their pelvic fins just touching the substrate. However, this leaves their eyes at least six inches above the rocks looking forward and up. We are not dealing with a bottom feeding fish such as carp or suckers.

So lighten up! Use less weight than you think you need to get to the bottom. An occasional tap will tell you that you are in the hitting zone. You'll hang up a lot less and hook more fish. Many times I've witnessed a line of drift anglers working a run below a fish concentrating dam or hatchery. One or two will be connecting regularly while the rest are left wondering why their eggs are being ignored. You can almost predict with your ears who the successful anglers are. Their is an audible "kaploosh" when the "on the bottom at all cost" anglers cast while you can't hear and can hardly see the terminal rigs of the pros enter the river. And, of course the unsuccessful anglers are frequently tugging at a snag or tying on new gear while the "lucky" ones keep casting, drifting and hooking.

Suspending Your Offering

Another way to keep your offering in the steelhead's strike zone without hanging up is through the use of a bobber. Overall bobbers are under utilized and many hard core bottom bouncers look down on the use of floats as too easy. They may even ask you how the bluegills are biting if they encounter you using a brightly colored piece of balsa or cork. But, the bottom line is that suspending your eggs or other bait under a bobber is a very effective way to fish any holding water, especially slow drifts and those with a tangle of snags on the bottom.

The success of the bobber and jig combination also helps demonstrate how steelhead will come up to grab a lure. Whether you are using a jig dressed with marbou or a real egg or wiggler, steelhead have been known to come up several feet to grab it in clear water. You can really get the steelies attention and increase the effectiveness of the jig by lightly jerking on the bobber causing the jig to rock and the marabou or wiggler's gill filaments to pulsate.

Lines and Leaders

Getting back to rigging your leaders should be at least a couple of pounds lighter in test than your mainline and made from a low visibility, fine diameter monofilament. A fluorescent mainline is fine for line watching but you don't want to spook a line-shy steelhead with a glowing leader.

The new, very high tensile strength gel-spun polyethylene braided lines can give you an edge when used for your mainline but are probably too visible to be used as a leader. Obviously the extra strength of these lines won't help in landing a steelhead hooked on a much lighter leader but they will save your swivel when you snag up. And, the fact that these lines are very sensitive and will telegraph pick-ups to you is a great advantage. Their lack of stretch helps when setting the hook and their fine diameter will decrease the tendency to belly in the current.

Try to keep your leaders relatively short. One to three feet should suffice in all but ultra clear water. Remember that sometimes you won't detect a pick-up until the sinker has bounced past the fish and stopped. With a five foot leader your sinker will have to travel ten feet before you know to set the hook and frequently the steelie will reject your offering during this time.

Attachment of a hook to your leader depends on the lure or bait you are using and the style of hook. Yarn and egg anglers want to snell their hook with an egg loop so the spawn sack, skein eggs or yarn can be slipped underneath. Of course, spawn sacks can be hooked directly and yarn tied on but most steelheaders think the loop does a better job of presenting the offering.

When using spinning drift baits such as the Spin-N-Glo and Birdie Drifter it is best to tie directly to a hook without a turned up eye and place a small plastic bead between the lure and hook. The bead acts as a bearing so the lure can spin easily.

Rigging Shortcuts

You can save rigging time when the rocks snatch your terminal tackle away by having leaders pretied to hooks and lures wrapped around leader cards in your vest. It is also a good idea to tie some with the swivel attached with a dropper line ready for the sinker in case everything is lost to a snag. This way all you have to do is attach the swivel to your mainline and squeeze on some lead and you're back in business.

Another way to reduce rigging time is to dispense with the swivel and leader all together. Simply tie on the hook and squeeze on the right amount of split shot a foot or two up the line. This method works best in high, dirty water where you can use fairly heavy line without spooking the steelies.

There is always some risk that the split shot may weaken the line but this problem can be reduced by putting a piece of rubber band along with the line in the split shot. The rubber will cushion the line and also make it so you don't have to squeeze the shot quite so hard to keep it in place. You can also loop a whole rubber band over your line like you would for a downrigger release and attach the split shot to the rubber band. Snug it up close to the line to minimize sliding.

Drift Tackle

The drift angler usually chooses a fairly long, limber rod with a parabolic or slow action to facilitate gentle casting of bait and to cushion light leaders against the surges and head shakes of strong steelhead. For most streams and types of drift fishing a length of nine to ten feet is about right. For large rivers and situations where keeping the line out of the current is important you may want to select rods in the 12 to 13 foot range. Float fisherman also often opt for the longer sticks.

Obviously sensitivity is very important to the bottom bouncer. Graphite is the logical first choice for a rod material because it does such a great job of transmitting vibrations. Graphite rod blanks seem to be in a continuous state of flux as the manufacturers strive for higher modulus and the resultant lighter and more sensitive rods. Standard graphite continues to perform well and is known for its

Joe Mazner battles a Fish Creek steelhead.

strength and durability. But there are many devotees to the more sensitive but somewhat fragile new generation of graphites.

Build or buy your rod with plenty of light weight, single foot ceramic guides and a handle set up that is comfortable. A rod equipped with a graphite reel seat, graphite arbors and a cork grip will maximize your ability to feel those subtle pick-ups.

Reels for drift fishing range from the traditional level winds to closed and open faced spinning to fancy center pin direct drive float reels. Choosing a reel for drift fishing is strictly a matter of personal preference. Since you will be fighting strong fish in heavy current with relatively light leaders a good drag system is important. The ability to feed line to extend your drift is facilitated by using level wind or bait casting reels with their free spool feature. The center pin reels were specifically designed to let that float continue downstream with no resistance.

Additional Tips

Drift anglers can increase their success by not getting locked into fishing one or two pet runs with only one lure or bait. If you are sure that fish are in front of you but you are not hooking up try a different bait or lure or color. Try different current lanes, cast further upstream or across and extend your drift by freespooling until your offering is almost to the brink of the next rapids. If there is uncertainty about steelhead being present in the holding water, move. Fish each run methodically but don't spend a long time at any one spot without action.

Remember, the keys to more effective drift fishing are to minimize rerigging time and to keep your offering near but not on the bottom. Look for more on drift techniques in the Being Prepared and Presentation chapters.

6

Plug Pulling

Diving, high action plugs are great steelhead finders and catchers. By teaming these lures with a drift boat you can cover more water, more efficiently than any other method.

Pulling plugs from a drift boat is commonly called Hot Shotting. The Hot Shot, for which the method is named, along with such lures as the Wiggle Wart, Tadpolly, Hot 'N Tot, Kwikfish, and Flatfish are frequent choices for this method of fishing. In reality, most any deep diving crankbait will do the job if the hooks are strong and sharp and the colors appeal to the steelhead.

The plugs are usually let out 50 to 60 feet behind the boat which is maneuvered so that the plugs wobble through the holding water. You are usually better off keeping the plugs fairly close to the boat but very clear water may require running them more than 60 feet back to keep from spooking the fish. Depending on the number of anglers on board and the allowable rods several lures can be run at one time. Most veteran Hot Shotters are careful to place each plug the same or a slightly staggered distance behind the boat so that the steelhead's territory is invaded over a wide area at the same time. Thus if the steelie moves to avoid an advancing plug it will immediately encounter another wobbling intruder. This frequently results in a very aggressive strike.

By varying the rate at which the boat is rowed against the current you can change the depth and amount of action your lures have. It is important to use the same lures or compatible plugs that have similar action and diving ability at the same current speed. The ease with which the drift boat can be maneuvered sideways helps you cover large holding pools in big rivers.

Dropping Plugs Back

Plugs can also be fished from an anchored boat but you must change plugs in order to vary the depth and lure action to match the river configurations. This is called dropback fishing and the key to success with this method lies with the selection of good fish holding water and proper positioning of your boat.

Taking angling current movements into account, anchor your boat upstream from the run to be fished. Anchor as quietly as possible to avoid alarming the steelhead. You may have to quickly pull anchor and follow a large, hooked steelie so a system should be worked out to handle this maneuver easily before that monster silver bullet dashes off downstream.

While dropback plugging is usually done from a boat this technique can also be used by the wading angler. Often you can wade out on a bar above a good run or work the plug from the bank on the outside of a bend.

Whether afloat or on foot let out some line into the current and hold. This forces the lure to dive against the flow and wiggle enticingly near the bottom. Continue to let out line and hold, let out and hold down through the run. Remember to choose highly visible plugs that have good action and dive near the bottom in the river section you are fishing.

The Take

Special rods have evolved for Hot Shotting and dropback fishing with plugs. Most are between seven and nine feet in length and have a magnum or extra fast taper from a light to medium tip to a very stiff butt section. A sensitive tip is very important to successful plug pulling whether you are watching it in a rod holder or have the rod in your hand. While plugs are known to elicit violent, "slam dunk" strikes from steelies many times the takes are much more subtle.

You should pay close attention to the vibration of the rod tip when the plug is wobbling normally. Steelhead may inhale the plug and swim along simply damping the vibrations or they may take the plug and move upstream causing the rod to straighten up and go motionless. Whenever there is a change set the hook. Most of the time a leaf, stick or some aquatic vegetation will be hanging on the lure but you sure don't want to miss a fish. Besides, even if it is not a steelie you need to get the fouled plug in and cleaned off so it will be effective.

Reel and Line

Level wind baitcasting reels are just right for plug pulling. The free spool mechanism is especially helpful when you are dropping back plugs from a stationary boat or wading position.

In the past Dacron line was used by guides specializing in dropback fishing. The reason was that the plugs were often worked well downstream from the boat and Dacron's lack of stretch facilitated the hook sets. The new braided lines also do not stretch very much and are made from stronger fibers (Kevlar and Spectra) thus the diameters are significantly smaller. These wispy lines can be a big plus in that they don't dampen the action of the lures as much as stiffer, larger diameter monofilament.

More Enticing

Another way to maximize the action of the plug is to make sure the lure is loosely attached to the line via a split ring or snap. Many of the diving plugs come equipped with one of these devices but if not you should add one rather than snugging a knot to the lure eye.

Usually the steelhead will be downstream from a plug and have a lot of time to examine the intruder. Adding scent to your lure can help the steelie find your offering, keep its attention and help convince the fish to hit it. Some western anglers actually wrap cut bait on the plug but I believe you can accomplish the same thing with scent and not affect the action or visibility of the lure. Use the gel types that last a long time.

Sticky Sharp and Other Terminal Concerns

While sharp hooks are important for all steelhead techniques they are especially critical when Hot Shotting. There will always be

Fred Eyer releases a steelhead hooked from an anchored boat.

time lags between hits and getting the hook set when the rods are in holders. Of course the steelies may hook themelves when they slam the plug but for soft hits you need the hooks to "stick" until you get the hook driven home.

Even though pulling plugs should cause less wear and tear on your line than other methods don't neglect to change it on a regular basis. Fresh, damage free line is important the way steelies nail the plugs. It is not much fun watching that steelhead jump with your plug dangling from its jaw, but not attached to your line any longer.

While the plug models you choose depend on the depth and current speed, the size and color selections are more related to river conditions. When the water is off color or turbid you should choose large plugs with bright fluorescent or contrasting colors. Pick plugs with rattles under these conditions to give steelies another reason to find and hit your lures. In Michigan some guides even take advantage of the law allowing two lures per line. Using a three way swivel they tie a smaller, shallow diving plug on the top leader and a deeper diving larger plug on the bottom to increase their chances of finding an aggressive steelhead.

In clear water smaller plugs in more subdued colors are preferred by most savvy plug pullers. Metallic finishes seem to be very effective with copper or copper in combination with other colors is a consistent favorite of many anglers. I've always been a bit skeptical of the phrase, the steelhead "preferred" such and such colors. It seems more logical to me that the steelhead may just be able to see a certain color better under those river and atmospheric conditions. But, regardless of the reason, if you find all or most of your hits are coming on one finish it makes sense to replace some of your unproductive models with the hot ones and not worry about why.

Be Versatile

When Hot Shotting the stick man is obviously doing all the fishing when the rods are in the holders. If you are pulling plugs in a drift boat with one or more partners you can increase your success by having them be active with the rods. By extending the rod far to the side of the boat they will often be able to get a plug closer to fish holding cover than you can by maneuvering the boat. In some situations such as a run with lots of fallen or overhanging trees you can back the plug underneath each by extending the rod but the multiple trees prevent you from rowing the boat along the bank.

Many anglers, especially in the Midwest, seem to have become enamored with Hot Shotting and ignore the versatility of the drift boat and how other techniques can be complimentary. You can greatly increase your chances for hookups on a drift by casting lures or drifting bait in addition to pulling plugs. In some states anglers are allowed two rods and you can keep the plugs working while casting into the pockets and slots along the edges of the river. Even if you are fishing in a one rod state at times you can reel in one of the plug rods and cast when the stream configuration suggests it.

Casting lures to the side may even attract steelhead to your plugs. Once I was casting spinners off the side of a drift boat where there were some submerged logs. I was watching the spinner so I could guide it between the logs when a steelhead began following it. The steelhead stayed with the spinner until it swung below the boat and then disappeared. Within seconds one of the plug rods slammed down. I will never be able to prove it but I believe that it was the same steelhead and it just happened to like plugs better than spinners.

A final thought—in addition to covering lots of water with

your Hot Shots try to take a different path than the other drift boats on popular rivers. In addition to showing your lures to new fish that are not in the prime holding water the other boats may have pushed fish out of the deeper runs and they are likely to be more aggressive when you come by. Of course, if your are the first boat down the river it pays not to neglect the best holding water.

7

Hardware Tossing

asting spoons and spinners is the most active method for catching steelhead. Both you and your lure are always on the move. Weighted spinners are my favorite lure for this technique, we will concentrate on them in this section. I think they are the ultimate flowing water lure. However, there are situations where spoons are superior and they can be used instead of spinners in any kind of water.

Even though this method is the least popular for steelhead I believe it is the most versatile. You can be effective with spinners in all types of holding water. It especially shines (sorry, bad pun) in water with lots of logs and other snags where it is difficult to get a good drift and there is not enough room to pull plugs.

If you bounce an egg cluster within a few inches of a steelhead's nose it is much more likely to grab it than a spinner flashed by just as close. However, a spawn bag drifted by three feet away from the steelie will go unnoticed while a flashing spinner may excite a strike from six feet.

Cover the Water

Therein lies the key to success when casting lures—cover lots of water retrieving or sweeping your shiny offering through as many holding areas as you can. Steelhead will usually strike a spinner on the first good pass so your goal will be to cover the water thoroughly and then move on to the next run. These lures are great attention getters, both visibly and sonically so you sure don't want to linger in runs that may not be holding fish. Fish the runs you have confidence in a little longer but the bottom line is keep moving.

When wading it is best to travel in an upstream direction. While steelhead are not as wary or streamwise as resident trout you will have a better chance of catching them if they don't know that you are there. Ironically, the most effective cast with a spinner is a cross or quartering downstream sweep. Thus it would appear that moving downstream would be more convenient. In large rivers and very fast rocky streams you can effectively wade and fish downstream. However, you should wade upstream in smaller rivers and almost always in slower moving streams with their sand and silt deposits in slack water areas.

The Casts

Casting upstream or quartering upstream and retrieving just fast enough to keep the blade turning is still a great way to catch steelies in narrow streams. Even though it seems like the spinner is traveling awfully fast downstream remember it is only moving slightly faster than the water and since the steelhead are in the same current they need to exert little effort to catch up to it. Casting upstream also makes it easy for you to get down to the fish. Try to cast to areas where you can retrieve your spinner past holding cover such as submerged logs and undercut banks.

Upstream casts with spinners should be reserved for days when there is plenty of clarity in the river. Three feet or more of visibility is a good guideline. Since you are retrieving the lure past the steelhead they need to see it in time to react.

Steelhead have a habit of following flashy lures. Always try to make your spinner change direction at the end of the retrieve at rod's length or further away. Let it swing around in the current before you bring it in and lift it from the water. This magic turn is frequently irresistible to following steelhead so be ready for a close quarters, smashing strike.

In general the more cross stream you make your cast the better as it gives the steelhead a longer look at the flashing lure. Stay to one edge of the stream and cast over into the holding water and let the lure sweep across the current.

Rainbows, whether they are ten inches or ten pounds, pounce on a lure that is hung in their face more than any other presentation. So, whenever possible sneak up on the shallow side of the stream and quarter downstream with your cast and let it hang in the current

Bright buck with a mouth full of metal.

moving as slowly across the flow as possible. Usually you will have to let the lure sink a bit first, don't pull too hard against the current or the spinner will start to rise against the resistance.

Just as you can extend your drift when bottom bouncing you can also extend your sweep with a spinner. Usually your spinner will start to rise when it gets directly below you. By giving line at a rate just slightly slower than the current speed you can keep the spinner down and moving downstream through the holding water.

You will soon develop a feel about how hard the river is tugging on the spinner and relate it to the kind of current that steelhead feel comfortable holding in. Keeping the spinner hanging in water that "feels right" and is close to cover is a real key to success. Don't waste time trying to get the spinner down in real fast water. Instead keep your spinner moving and probe those fast flows for slacker water caused by an obstruction and when you find it get ready for a jolting strike.

Spinner Watching

In relatively small, clear streams you will frequently be able to follow your spinner with your eyes because of its high visibility. Watching your spinner will help guide it close to fish holding in brush and root wads without hanging up. If you can keep from getting buck fever it will add to your hookups when that gray torpedo appears behind the lure and takes it very gently.

One time I was taking a break from a drift boat ride down Oregon's Nehalem River and wandered up a feeder stream that was also open to fishing. In the second pool up from the main river a large fish followed my spinner but did not take. Because I knew there was a fish present I kept casting the pool and sneaked up alongside to get a different angle on the holding water.

Suddenly the fish appeared again behind the spinner. Quick as a camera flash I saw the white of the steelhead's open mouth and no more spinner. I felt absolutely nothing but managed to keep my wits about me and set the hook. After a lengthy tug of war including freeing my line from around a boulder I had my second largest Oregon steelhead, a 17 1/2 pound buck lying on its side in the shallows. We will talk more about detecting subtle hits but in this case you had to see it to have a chance.

Even when you can't follow your spinner very well because of depth or clarity you should still keep your eyes open in the general path of the lure if only to watch for possible snags. Being observant may also pay dividends in other ways. For example, I was quickly making my way through some marginal holding water on Michigan's Betsie River when I thought I saw a subtle flash under the water. So I peppered the relative shallow run with more casts and saw the muted flash several more times. Finally I felt a strange drag on the lure and set the hook into a large steelhead that wanted to go downstream in a hurry. It was a fun chase and a happy ending for the angler. This was obviously a situation where the steelhead needed some extra coaxing but was not a prime spot where I would normally have made multiple casts. But keeping my eyes peeled through the polarized glasses paid off.

Rigging and Line Twist

Rigging up with a spinner is extremely simple. You just attach it directly to your line with your favorite monofilament knot. My preference is the trilene knot but the similar improved clinch knot and the palomar knot also work well. You want a knot that is about 90 percent of the line strength so if you do have to break off on a snag you won't leave any line in the river. When tying on a spoon you will want to make sure your lure is equipped with a split ring or sturdy snap for loose attachment and resultant better action. But for spinners snug directly to the shaft since the action is in the revolving blade.

Many of you may be wondering about line twist but I have always fished weighted spinners without a swivel. You can prevent line twist by giving the blade a chance to reverse direction by stopping and starting the retrieve or allowing it to tick the bottom. For extra insurance against line twist lift the revolving lure from the water with six to eight feet of line off the rod tip and allow it to untwist for a moment before reeling up near the tip for the next cast.

Which Models

There are many spinner types available which is very helpful since rivers are ever changing in both current speed and depth. By selecting blade sizes and body weights it is possible to match the conditions.

In general, the narrower the blade, the closer it will revolve to the body and the faster it must be retrieved in order to spin properly. This is because the narrow blade has less resistance to the water. The narrow-bladed spinner will also travel deeper because of this lower resistance.

Because they spin at a very slow retrieve I prefer to use spinners with the broad "French" domed blade. For some fast water situations I will switch to narrower in-line spinners for downstream sweeps but most of the time I pitch French spinners with varying body weights.

In the past I've preached using the largest, gaudiest spinner possible up to the point of spooking the steelhead instead of exciting these fish into striking. In recent years I've had more success using a spinner that tends to be smaller but is still very visible and gets down to the fish. Matching the river conditions and size and brightness of the day continues to be the key to selecting the right spinner or spoon.

The advantage goes to heavy compact spoons when the water is especially deep or fast or you need to cast a long way. Highly curved spoons stamped from solid brass are best for steelhead and they should be fished on quartering downstream casts and swept against the current to get maximum action at a slow retrieve. Silver

Author with spinner-caught 15 pound hen.

combined with bright fluorescent colors will get the steelhead's attention.

Make 'em Visible

For maximum visibility with both spinners and spoons you should choose real silver as this metal reflects light much better than nickel or chrome. For bright days and clear water switch to a smaller spinner or if you still need a larger model to reach the fish switch to brass. Adding fluorescent tape to the back of the blade allows the spinner to retain its maximum flash while making the inside of the blade much more visible from behind the lure. It also causes the spinner to change from silver to a bright color when it makes that magic turn in front of a fish.

The Gear

Fairly heavy line can be used when tossing hardware because of the attention the lure gets. By choosing high tensile strength thin monofilament lines you can employ 12 to 17 pound test and still cast your spinners well. While usually not necessary to land steelhead the stout line will give you a chance when the fish goes under a log or around a rock. And, it will help you pull your lures off the snags.

On long sweep casts in large rivers there is almost always a belly in the line and this along with the stretch in mono can make good hook sets difficult. You need to haul back on the rod. Using the new braided lines with virtually no stretch can really increase your hooking percentage when making long casts.

While level wind reels are preferred by most steelheaders for drift fishing and plug pulling I strongly feel that spinning reels are best for lure tossing. Lots of short, accurate casts need to be made when spinner fishing and it is difficult to get the spool revolving on a level wind for these little flips of relatively light lures. A quality, medium freshwater, open faced spinning reel with a fast retrieve ratio and super smooth gearing is just the ticket for spinner fishing. A good drag is also important when dealing with line sizzling steelies unless you are weird like me and back reel instead of using the drag.

Backlashes are not a problem with spinning reels but loops can impede your steelheading. The loops form on the reel spool when there is slack in your line when the bail is flipped. Some twist in your line, along with the slack, will increase the chance of a loop being laid down on the spool. To prevent loops, lift your rod as you engage the bail. This action will take the slack out of your line and prevent most loops from forming. You can also stop the cast by closing the bail and this will prevent loops.

A relatively short, seven to eight foot, rod with a light tip and a fast taper to a stiff butt section is ideal for spinner tossing. Sensitive graphite is important because it lets you feel the spinner revolving. Even though steelies often clobber the flashy lure, their take can also be subtle and you must set the hook any time the spinner doesn't feel right. I generally use a seven foot rod for small streams and a seven and a half in good sized rivers. Since I build them with very short (2-3 inch) butt grips they are really equivalent to 7 1/2 and 8 foot factory rods.

Close, But Not Too Close

A frequently repeated saying (I've already repeated it in this volume) about steelheading states that if you aren't hanging up on the bottom a lot you are not fishing right. The idea being that you need to be dragging the bottom and the cover to catch these fish. When I go spinner fishing my goal is to "almost snag up" on every cast. The perfect presentation passes your lure very close to the logs and rocks without ever hanging up. Of course perfect casts everytime are impossible but are still a good goal.

While you will hang up a lot less casting spinners than bottom bouncing it is important not to worry about losing a few lures. When you're fishing just to save spinners you won't catch many steelhead. "Snag phobia" is easier to overcome when the lures are costing less than 40 cents. There are lots of high quality commercial spinners on the market that work well for steelhead but you can make your own that are even better and are customized to the river you are fishing.

Making Spinners

A special feature of this lure is that they are very easy for you to make. You just have to assemble the component parts with no painting, carving or other effort that might require some special talent. Below you will find details on building high quality weighted spinners with just a pair of needle nose pliers.

The blade, body, shaft and hook are the four principal components of a weighted spinner. As already discussed probably the best all-round blade for weighted spinners for river fishing is the domed "French" type. However some river anglers prefer the in-line blade and these became available to the lure crafter a few years ago.

The French blade is now available in seven sizes and with nickel, brass, copper and silver finishes. Black nickel, chrome or blades painted with a large variety of fluorescent colors can also be purchased. Some suppliers have these blades with hammered surfaces in addition to the smooth finishes. There is an even larger variety of bodies made from brass, lead and plastic.

Rather than describing all of the possible blade, body and hook matchups let's get started on making a size four spinner which is the size I use most often for steelhead. First place fluorescent vinyl or latex tubing on the shank of a size two treble hook. Hang the hook on the loop of a preformed open wire shaft and close the loop by sliding on a large brass body over both wires. Add a smaller brass body and a five millimeter plastic bead for a total body length of about 26 mm. See the chart for suggested body lengths for all sizes but these can be altered as long as the hook does not interfere with the spinning of the blade. Having the blade hang down to the eye of the treble hook is ideal.

Now we are ready to hang a number four blade on a clevis and slide it onto the shaft with the concave side toward the hook. Using needle nosed pliers with parallel grooves (not cross hatches) make a right angle bend in the shaft about 5/8 of an inch from the clevis (see diagram). Then move the pliers just the width of the needle nose closer to the clevis and make another right angle bend (2). Place the squared off end in the jaws of the pliers and squeeze. This will cause the wires to cross and round the loop (3). Now wrap the wire one and a half times around the shaft and trim off the end (4). Align the loop so that it is directly in line with the spinner shaft and you are ready to go fishing. The loop should end up about 1/8 of an inch from the clevis which will allow the blade to easily spin yet will be close enough so the bodies can't slide up and open up the shaft freeing the hook.

Sizes three, five and six are made similarly to the size four with changes in the size and number of plastic beads. One 3 mm bead is used on the three, three 4 mm beads on the five and three 5 mm beads on the size six.

Lead bodies can be employed with the larger blades to make heavier spinners. I have found that using 1/4 ounce worm weights adds just enough heft to the spinner to get it down to the bottom in those fast, deep runs where steelhead like to hang out. Heavier worm weights can be used but if you use too heavy a body the spinner will not spin well.

On a number five place an 8 mm bead on the double wire first and then slide on a worm weight followed by two 4 mm beads. The size six is made the same way except for using two 5 mm beads below the blade. For a number four place a 6 mm bead below the lead body and 5 mm bead above it. Lead bodies can be purchased already painted or you can paint your own with special jig paints. Always use a white base coat under any fluorescent or luminescent paint.

Smaller models are built slightly differently because of the smaller base body. For a size one spinner you should bend over and clip off the extra wire after you have slipped on the 1/16 ounce brass body. Next slide on a small bearing bead followed by a 3/16 inch solid brass bead and the blade and the clevis. The size zero

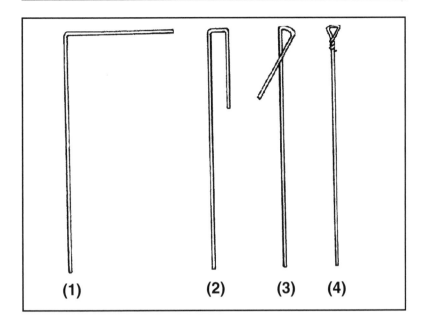

(1)	**(2)**	**(3)**	**(4)**

spinner is made the same way except that a 7/32 inch solid brass bead is used instead of the 1/16 ounce brass body. The size two and a light weight size three are made using the 1/16 ounce body, a smaller "T" brass body and one 4 or 5 mm bead respectively.

When building in-line spinners you will need to make the loop a bit further up the shaft away from the blade to allow it to revolve around the shaft freely. Because of this it is best to close the loop around the hook on larger spinners rather than burying the short end of the open shaft in a large body. Otherwise there is the potential for the body to slide up and release the hook while you are fighting a fish.

You can customize your spinner blades by applying lure tape. Witchcraft Tape Products (Box 937, Coloma, MI 49038), makes a wide variety of self-adhesive tapes specifically for fishing lures including die cuts sized just right for spinner blades. Use two contrasting colors of fluorescent tape for maximum visibility and put it on the back of the blade for the reasons discussed earlier. Be sure to wipe the blade clean and dry before applying the tape and put it on with lots of pressure. The rounded end of a ball point pen cover works well to press down the tape. Use two contrasting colors of tubing to make your spinner even more gaudy.

There are a number of companies that can supply spinner components. The following have catalogs and a good selection of parts. Netcraft (2800 Tremainsville Rd., Toledo, OH 43613); Cabela's (812 - 13th Ave., Sidney, NE 69160)—note: their French blades are sized one number larger than the others, eg., their size four is really a size three. In addition their regular French blades are too thin in the large sizes so be sure and choose their "heavy" French blades in sizes 3-5; Angling Specialties (19520 McLoughlin Blvd., Gladstone, OR 97027)—note: they have special matte silver plated blades that work well in stained or muddy water and their own custom bodies; Pen Tac (P.O. Box 18273, Seattle, WA 98118)—note: they have thicker blades and special large brass bodies for downstream sweep casts in fast, deep water; and Fisherman's Shack (9465 Airlie Rd., Monmouth, OR 97361).

Custom Spinners

BLADE SIZE	-0-	-1-	-2-	-3-	-4-	-5-	-6-
Hook Size	10	8	6	4	2	2	2
Body Length, mm	11	13	17	21	26	33	37

8

Wading Techniques

Pulling on chest waders and walking up the stream is my favorite way to try to hook the king of the river. Fishing on foot allows you to approach steelhead quietly, keeping them unaware of your presence. And, when you hook a fish you are there in its element, often getting a close up look and a shower from the re-entry splash.

Many steelhead anglers feel limited when they are not in a jet or drift boat. It is true that much of the holding water in most of our larger rivers can only be reached when afloat. By the same token there are more smaller rivers that either have too many shallow areas, log jams or brush for a boat. A good number of rivers can be drifted when the water is up but are best waded when they drop and clear.

Most anglers on foot wear waders or hip boots just to keep dry while they stand at the edge of a pool or run close to an access point. You can improve your success by actively wading up to several miles away from the access site on your outings. While you can't travel as far as a drift boat in a day you can cover the water more carefully and get to parts of the river that are not being fished as hard. And, at least in the west, it is much more common to see a parade of drift boats than wading anglers.

Wading Staff

An almost required piece of equipment when you're wading from one access point to another is a sturdy wading staff. It will help you cross the river and wade through fast flowing or deep sections of river. Your staff acts as both a third leg for stability in strong

The author using a wading staff in Oregon's Smith River.

currents and as a probe to find out what is ahead. When crossing the river in fast flows keep the staff on your upstream side and lean into it. If the staff is below you the current can readily lift it up off the bottom which could cause you to lose your balance and get wet.

For deep water or unseen obstacles in turbid rivers the staff can also serve as searching tool. Making your wading staff about as long as your waders are tall will let a wet hand indicate that you are getting close to using up all of your available freeboard.

To the upper end of your wading staff attach a cord so you can tie it to your wader belt or vest and let it float behind you when not in use. Be sure and make the attachment at the end because if you drill a hole down the staff a few inches you create a "Vee" with the cord and end of the staff that is guaranteed to catch on stream side brush.

Wading staffs can be purchased or made from a sturdy broom or garden tool handle. Ash, hickory and other hardwood saplings about an inch or so in diameter make excellent staffs. Ski poles and hockey sticks without the blade also can be used. In addition to facilitating safe wading and river crossings the staff can help you get in and out of the river when the bank is high, steep and slippery.

Staying Dry

Submerged boulders and logs, clay and bedrock ledges, fast current, deep water and an uneven stream bottom are the main obstacles to the safe wading of our steelhead rivers. The cardinal rule that will keep you dry when wading is to always have two parts of the tripod securely planted before you move the third one.

When wading in strong current keep sideways in the flow to minimize water resistance. Always move with a shuffle step so that your legs never become crossed. Keep in mind that your center of gravity is at your hips so you must take care that the current doesn't tip you over when wading deeper. Never wade deeper than your waist unless the current is very gentle.

When preparing to cross a river with a swift current try to pick a route that heads both across and down. This will keep you from having to fight the current as you wade to the other side. It is also helpful to pick a crossing location that is at the upper end of a shallow area so if the current does push you downstream a bit you will still have plenty of time and room to get to the other bank.

Closely watching where you are wading should be a given but this is certainly a key to keep from stumbling over a big rock or log. Your polarized sunglasses will play a big role in helping spot underwater obstacles. Pay attention to breaks or bulges in the surface current as they will also indicate boulders and submerged logs. If the water is muddy you must wade slower making doubly sure that you have your wading staff and one boot firmly planted before you move the other.

In fact, slowing down is a good way to stay dry under any conditions. A fishing buddy of mine has the well deserved nickname of "crash" because he is always in a hurry and an eventual dive seems to happen on most trips. We even threaten to carry score cards so we can appropriately evaluate his entry into the river. Longer, slower steps are also quieter and less likely to alert the steelhead to your presence.

Selecting Waders

Neoprene waders are the first choice of most ardent steelheaders especially in the fall, winter and spring. The two biggest advantages of neoprene waders are that they stretch and they provide excellent insulation against the cold water. Because they stretch they can be made to be form fitting which results in much less drag in the water. Perfect for the active wading steelheader.

In general the Great Lakes area steelheader usually chooses boot foot waders while the Pacific Northwest angler commonly dons the stocking foot model. The sturdy wading shoe protects the western angler from the ever present large rocks while in the midwest we are frequently dealing with frigid water temperatures and the boot foots are much warmer. Water pressure squeezes the sock around your feet resulting in cold feet while the rigid insulated boot traps more air keeping you toasty. You can help keep your feet warm with stocking foot neoprenes by purchasing wading shoes an extra size larger and wearing neoprene socks inside and outside the waders. My problem is that with my oversized feet I can barely find a large enough wading shoe to fit over just a 3 mm wader.

Boot Soles

Regardless of whether you choose boot foot or stocking foot a decision must be made on the type of sole for the boot or wading shoe that will be help you maneuver on your favorite streams. If the substrate is usually sand and small gravel then cleated rubber soles will suit you fine. When slippery, algae covered rocks line your most frequent haunts then you should pick boots with felt soles. They will give you much better traction on the relatively smooth, slippery bedrock found on the bottom of many western steelhead rivers.

A disadvantage with felt soles is that snow and mud tend to cling to them. Many times I've ventured out with the ground bare only to get dumped on by the white stuff. When the snow is wet you will soon grow much taller making walking very difficult. Of course, if you are quick this might be an advantage when trying to cross a deep section of the river.

For my Great Lakes tributary fishing the solution has been to purchase rubber soled waders and a pair of sandals equipped with metal cleats. Then when the rocks are slippery I strap on the cleats. The cleated sandals also work well when there is a lot of shelf ice but are not so hot on snow.

Warm Weather Wading

For summer steelheading light weight but tough cordura nylon waders are just the ticket for me. Many steelheaders stick with neoprene boots all year but when the air temperature is in the 80s and the water in the 60s it is time to give the foam waders a rest. Some anglers try to get by with hip boots in the summer and on small streams, but I believe they are too limiting. Even if you rarely wade above your knees on a stream there will always be those times when you need to be standing in deep water or kneeling in order to be in the right position to make the best presentation of your offering. Of course if it is really warm and the water is not too frigid you can just forget the waders. It is still a good idea to wear your wading shoes to protect your feet and long pants are better than shorts when the mosquitos are out.

Good Fit

As an active wading steelheader you must make sure that your waders fit well. The critical area is the leg length and fit in the crotch. A good test is to lift your knee above the waist. If there is no binding then you should be able to get in and out of the stream and climb over the logs. Be cautious about getting a pair with the legs too long, however. You will have plenty of movement freedom but the extra bagginess will add water resistance and you will soon be chafing holes in the inseam area around the knees.

It is better to have the boots a little large than too snug. Try the waders on wearing the socks that you would wear fishing and then leave room for one more pair and they will be just right. If they are too tight your blood circulation will be cut off and your feet will get cold even if the boots are well insulated.

Wader Care

A good pair of waders are a sizable investment so it is important to take good care of them. Always dry out the inside after each outing. This is easy with stocking foots as you can just turn them inside out. With boot foots the task is more difficult. There are special wader dryers but I utilize one of the old fashioned bonnet type hair dryers with the bonnet removed from the hose. Usually a non-fishing friend or relative has one sitting idle on the shelf or you may have to hit the garage sale circuit. After drying, neoprene waders should be stored upright on a broad hanger with the boots resting on the floor to keep from unnecessarily stretching the foam. This also allows any residual water to escape as water vapor is lighter than air (a good reason for not hanging boots upside down). Keep them away from sunlight, heat and ozone generating electric motors.

Wader Repair

Eventually you will wear a hole in your waders, a seam will start to seep or you will have an unfortunate encounter with a blackberry vine, sharp beaver stub or barbed wire. There are a multitude of patching materials available but as I write this the most versatile and effective is a product called Aquaseal. This is a very flexible and tough urethane rubber compound with super adhesive properties.

No additional patch is needed even for rips and holes. Simply back the damaged area with a removable tape such as masking tape. Tape the tear or hole keeping the wader material in its original position with no puckers. Make sure the area is clean and dry and on a flat surface.

Squeeze some Aquaseal onto the damaged area and spread it with a flat stick. The urethane compound will level itself and will run if you don't keep the repaired area flat during curing. The repair will reach full strength in about 24 hours but I've made repairs the night before and not had problems. If the hole or rip is quite large you may want to reinforce the "patch" by applying the compound to the other side after removing the tape.

On Stream Patching

An accelerator called Cotol-240 can be used if a quick cure is needed and is now available in a small bottle which you can carry in your vest. Aquaseal has the special feature of sticking to wet waders so it works well for on stream repair when used with the accelerator.

Wading anglers enjoy a leaping steelhead.

If you poke a hole in the leg of your neoprenes there is another way to survive the rest of the day. On a cold January day I had an unfortunate encounter with a sharp beaver stub hidden under the snow. Luckily I was still close to the car and had a spare pair. Quickly I returned, changed and hustled back upstream as I had already hooked two steelhead. You guessed it, another sharp stick. Now what do I do? The steelies are turned on but there is no way I can endure 32 degree water flowing freely in and out of my boots. Well, I had a heavy duty rubber band keeping my net bag off the ground so I doubled over the damaged spot used the rubber band to hold it in place. The self sealing qualities of the neoprene kept the leak down to a very slow seep and I was able to keep exercising the steelies all day.

Preventive maintenance will also add life to your waders. Check your waders frequently for wear spots and put a thin layer of sealant over the area that shows signs of abrasion before the hole develops. You can also add life to your felt soles by putting a narrow strip of Aquaseal along the edge of the heal and toe where the felt seems to wear off prematurely.

So don't lament the next time the water is too low to launch your drift boat. Pull on your boots and go for a pleasant walk in the water, the fish will still be there and they won't have been hassled by a parade of boats. Likewise, if your favorite bank hole has too many cars parked in the pull off try wading upstream and you may find even better holding water with undisturbed steelies.

9

Hooking, Playing, Landing & Releasing

One of the reasons that steelhead are revered as special trophies of the piscatorial world is that hooking one does not guarantee a fish on the beach. So many of these hard fighting fish get away that many anglers measure their success in hook-ups rather than steelies brought to hand. Only landed steelies make it into my log book, however, so I work hard to capture each anadromous rainbow that I hook.

A good hook set is key to keeping steelies on the end of your line until you can corral them. As described previously in the methods chapters successful hook-ups start with sharp hooks and having a rod with enough stiffness to drive it home. Obviously, a small sharp single egg hook is easier to bury past the barb than a large treble on a lure so a limber rod can still be used for drift fishing.

A Tight Rein

Once the steelie is hooked solidly your goal should be to try to stay close to the fish and maintain some control. The operative word here is "try" since fresh run steelhead often go berserk and defy you to control them in any way.

Follow after the fish whenever possible, especially when it heads downstream. The shorter the line between you and the silver battler the better. Don't try to pump a steelhead back upstream unless that is the only alternative as fighting both the current and the fish greatly cuts down the odds on landing it. A definite error is to try to pressure a steelie against the current when it is rolling and thrashing on the surface. And, don't try to stop a steelhead making a mad dash toward a big stump but rather try and steer the fish away from it.

If you can't follow the fish try to finesse it into swimming back upstream. This is usually accomplished by slacking off on the pressure on the fish and, in desperate situations, stripping line into the current making the steelhead think its adversary is now pulling from below.

Once you have gained some control of the fish and are across from it you should not let the steelie rest. Rod pressure low to the water drawing the fish sideways in the current toward the shore is especially effective. Just maintaining the status quo with your rod held high and the fish holding its position in the center of the river prolongs the fight. This gives the hook more time to wear a hole and pull free and may exhaust the fish to the point it can't recover.

The Landing

As your prize tires your next goal is to get below it and look for a landing area. I prefer to use a big landing net and try to get out of the main current while staying in thigh to waist deep water. This allows me to capture the steelie when it is still a bit green which enhances its chance for survival when released. If you try to pressure the steelhead into shallow water it will often spook and take off on another run bringing it closer to exhaustion.

Tired steelie beached in shallow water.

Most western steelheaders prefer to beach their fish while the relative lack of shallow bars keeps a good number of Great Lakes anglers carrying nets. Some have the opinion that the net cords abrade the surface of the fish and rub off protective slime and scales. I think that if you keep the net bag in the water while unhooking the fish the mucus loss will be slight. While minimal handling is best, if you have to tire a fish until it is quiet enough for you to grab the hook with pliers without the net or holding the steelie, it may not recover.

In some instances it is possible to put a steelhead on shore faster than you can net it when an appropriate beach or gravel bar is present. But, it is quite likely the fish may injure itself flopping on the rocks or ground. In addition the sand can be very hard on their slime coating. A fish to be released should not be pulled up the bank above the water line.

The ideal beaching situation occurs when you have a shallow area where the steelhead can be forced on its side but still has a couple inches of water to cushion it. Under these conditions you can usually unhook and slide the fish back into deeper water quickly with little handling.

TLC

All handling of steelhead should be minimal and as gentle as possible. It is a good idea to try to avoid the gill and eye areas as they are very sensitive to damage. However, it is possible to slide your fingers inside the gill cover without disturbing them and this may be helpful in providing leverage when trying to remove a particularly stubborn hook. This takes a practiced hand and you should try to unhook the steelhead without this maneuver if possible.

I firmly believe that needlenosed pliers or sturdy hemostats or forceps should be required equipment for all steelhead and other salmonid anglers. All of these fish have sharp teeth and these tools allow removal of hooks with minimal damage to both the fish and the fisherman. Trying to twist out a hook manually usually means sliced up fingers and a steelhead with internal damage from squeezing or being dropped on the ground or boat floor.

If you hook a steelie in the gills or deep in the gullet when using single hooks that are not attached to a spoon or plug it is best to just cut your line. When fishing with eggs, sand shrimp or other

Joe Mazner "beaches" a steelhead on an ice shelf.

bait select hooks that will rust easily. Avoid using stainless steel hooks and those plated for saltwater use.

For lures, do the best you can with your pliers to back the hook out. Sometimes it is possible to cut the hook with side cutters or diagonal pliers rather than chancing removal. If you do have to try to remove the hook remember that it is usually easiest to back it out the same way it went into the steelhead's mouth. This will often mean that you have to push deeper into their mouth to free it. Pressing the hook down will also help make room for the barb to pass out with minimal damage.

If the steelhead does bleed profusely either during the battle or hook removal you have probably broken a gill artery and you should retain the fish if it is legal to do so because it will not survive. Fish have a small amount of blood compared to birds and mammals and the loss of even an ounce or two will usually be fatal. A small amount of blood from the mouth area should cause no problems and you can release the steelhead with confidence that it will continue its journey to the spawning gravel.

If you frequently experience difficulty with hook removal you may want to consider using barbless hooks or manually flattening the barbs with pliers. Sometimes just pinching down the barb partially or using hooks with small barbs will do the trick and you will still have some holding power when that silver acrobat starts to jump and shake its head.

During the time that you are handling a steelhead it is important to keep it in the water as much as possible so that oxygen will continue to be available to the fish. If you are struggling with a particularly stubborn hook-up, periodically lower the fish back under the water as you work to free the lure. Likewise if you are weighing or photographing your catch don't keep it out of the water for more than a minute or so.

The Release

Steelhead should always be released in an area where the river current is slow. If your fish appears exhausted or is disoriented hold it upright facing into a gentle current. This will allow water to flow over the gills and should revive the steelie. Do not move it back and forth as the backward movement is counterproductive. If there is no current try moving it forward in a circle or walk with the steelhead. When the fish begins to struggle it is usually ready to take off on its own. If the water temperature is below 60 degrees and you landed the steelie quickly they will usually jump out of your hands with no need for resuscitation.

The Reward

Every steelheader can help ensure the future of the sport by releasing these great game fish. Obviously, releasing wild steelhead where they have reproduced successfully for many generations is especially important. In situations where hatchery fish do not adversely effect wild fish letting them go provides opportunities for more anglers to enjoy them and may take some of the angling pressure off the wild steelhead.

Sometimes you can reap personal benefits almost immediately by recycling steelies. I had had a real successful day for summer steelhead two days earlier with six fish landed up to 14 pounds so I

The author releases a large silver buck.

was back hoping for a repeat of the fine action. As is often the case it was not to be and after five hours of no hits I was getting discouraged. Just as I was about to give in to the skunk, a large gray form glided out from a mass of roots at the tailout of the bend hole. The white mouth opened and my spinner disappeared. With little room to fight the fish we went toe to fin for about a minute with water flying everywhere. I was soaked but the prize was in the net. Upon a closer look I discovered that I had landed, marked and released the same 13 pound hen from the upper part of the bend on my previous trip.

If I hadn't returned that fish it would have been a no encounter trip. We can all decrease our empty outings in the years to come for ourselves and our children by releasing most of the steelhead we catch.

10

When the Going Gets Tough

Every steelheader yearns to be on the river when conditions are just right. The level is falling and a fresh run of bright steelies is settling into their new habitat. The water is clear but not too clear—there is still mystery to the runs and holes—"steelhead green" they call it on many rivers.

Well, most of us have job and family demands and a fair distance to travel to get to our favorite steelhead haunts. We go when we can and the river conditions are only occasionally ideal. Or, if you chase steelhead often you are certain to find at times the rivers to be too high and muddy, too icy, too warm, too low and clear,

A bobber was used to get a hookup in low water.

etc. You can still be successful under these adverse conditions by adapting your methods and changing streams.

Each winter I travel to Oregon for about 10 days to fish coastal streams with a long-time fishing buddy. When I first started making these annual treks I soon gained the reputation of being a magnet for big storms off the Pacific. For five or six years in a row some of the heaviest rains of the winter would douse the coast during my short visit. For a while I was even thinking about giving up my regular job and hiring out as a full time traveling drought buster.

Despite the high, muddy water I had traveled to fish for steelhead and obviously couldn't wait for better conditions. So we did lots of driving and usually found marginally fishable water and caught some steelies. In fact one year over nine inches of rain fell during a three day storm and the only day I did not fish was when a mud slide closed the road to the only small stream that wasn't opaque.

Chocolate Milk

When heavy rains muddy your favorite rivers and your scheduled trip can't be postponed you can either try to find streams less affected by the runoff, change tactics or both. As you can probably gather from the above I tend to persevere with the spinner tossing and try to find creeks with enough clarity.

Usually your best chance to find streams with better visibility is to move up to the headwaters. The further upstream you go the faster the river will recover from the runoff and the more likely you will find clear tributaries. With time you will also develop a repertoire of streams that are minimally effected by runoff such as watersheds with no clear cutting or agricultural runoff or streams that have sandy soils that soak up most of the rain.

While clear tributary spawning creeks may be closed to fishing they will often create a clearer band of water along the edge of the main river. Add to this the fact that steelhead tend to travel and rest close to shore during high water periods and you have a great place to fish. Concentrate on keeping your offering in the clear water/dirty water interface as long as possible with each drift or cast. This is usually easier to accomplish by fishing on the clear creek side of the river.

If you can't find water that isn't high and muddy it is time to try relatively stationary techniques in areas where steelies are likely to be concentrated. Plunking with a smorgasbord of eggs or sand shrimp coupled with a large action drift bait (Spin-N-Glo, Birdie, Wobbleglo, etc.) below a dam, weir, water fall or hatchery may produce when conditions seem impossible. A large, bright fluorescent plug with a rattle very slowly inched downstream will often draw some interest from a steelhead.

It is important to change from concentrating on your favorite deep runs and pools to the pocket water along the edges of the river when the water is raging. Not only will there be few fish in the holes but it will be almost impossible for any that are present to find your offering. Look for slower water and a place where a boulder or log breaks the current along the streambank. The turbidity provides cover so the fish can lay in two or three feet of water.

Gin Clear

After weeks of cold weather and no rain most steelhead rivers become low and ultra clear. When this happens there is no problem figuring out where the fish are laying. You just have to convince them to come out of hiding and take your lure or bait. Sometimes I

Kneeling helps keep anglers from spooking fish when water is low and clear.

could swear the steelies have their pectoral fins wrapped around their eyes when the sun is out and the water is crystal clear.

As discussed in earlier chapters steelhead are cover oriented and this becomes even more pronounced when the river is low and clear. The fish tend to get spooky and become reluctant to move out of heavy cover to continue to migrate upstream or to take your offering.

Now you should concentrate your efforts on those streams that have lots of cover and plenty of deep runs. Larger rivers will usually produce better than the creeks. Try those streams that are last to clear and still have a little bit of lingering color or turbidity. In the Great Lakes area give those streams that are always stained with tannins more effort when most of the rivers are low and translucent.

It is also time to use lighter line and smaller lures or single eggs instead of clusters coupled with drift bobbers. If you are Hot Shotting you will want to increase the amount of line you have out and use smaller, less gaudy plugs. A stealthy upstream approach will pay off best for the wading angler because if the steelhead become aware of your presence they will be unlikely to hit.

If the sun is out I always try to fish river sections that are flowing east and west with lots of high banks and tall evergreens lining the banks. This maximizes my chances of finding the holding water in the shade where it is much more likely that you can entice a steelie to come out and strike. In the west move from your favorite drifts near tidewater up into the canyons where you often have perpetual shade in the winter.

In low clear water use lures with less flash and watch them closely. The shy steelies will often take the lure very softly and quickly reject it so if you are watching you have a much better chance at a hookup.

Ice Floes and Shelves

Steelhead are amazing fish in that they remain active in very cold water temperatures. On one frigid morning we encountered a river narrowed by shelf ice and clogged with floating floe ice. The water was below 32 degrees and anchor ice coated the bottom of the riffles. Ice had to be removed from my spinner after each cast and from the rod guides almost as often. It was ridiculously cold and I was ready to surrender when the spinner seemed to hang up.

*Battling both the steelhead and the ice in Michigan's
Pere Marquette River.*

Despite my numbed senses I set the hook and felt the wonderful throb of a big steelie. The adrenalin rush was a great way to warm up and four more steelhead made me forget about the cold that day.

Even if the steelies don't mind the icewater you will fish more effectively if you don't have to battle the ice, both in the river and clinging to your tackle. Moving to rivers less likely to have icy conditions is a good plan unless the half frozen river is known to have a lot more fish. I can tolerate much colder weather when I know the river water will be at least 33 degrees so I know my lure won't ice up and I can stick my rod tip in the flow to de-ice the guides.

In the Great Lakes region, where you are most likely to experience ice problems, fishing below a dam is a good choice when the arctic air settles in. Even relatively low head dams will have open water below them because the river freezes solid above them and the ice insulates the water from the cold air. Streams with high groundwater contributions to their flow will stay open in the areas where the major springs are located even when the mercury hovers near zero for several days. In the west cold snaps are less frequent and you can usually move to lower elevations or toward the coast and find open water.

If you can't avoid the ice floes and it's your only chance to chase steelies for awhile then there are some tactics that will help you overcome the elements. If you plan to drift fish it is definitely time to break out the floats. When ice floes are present it becomes almost impossible to bottom bounce conventionally. With a bobber all you have to do is cast into an opening in the ice and then let the bobber float along with the ice. Even when there isn't any floe ice your cold hands and frequent exposure to raw winds make detecting strikes difficult when bottom bouncing.

The Hot Shotter can take a page out of the troller's repertoire and utilize downriggers to prevent ice from sliding down the line and fouling the plugs. Just set the downriggers a foot or so below the surface and back your way downstream as usual. Utilizing the new very low stretch braided polyethylene lines should be especially helpful in this case in getting good hook sets.

For the lure tosser concentrating on using heavy, compact spoons instead of spinners will help you get to the fish when the water is on the thick side. In addition to diving through floe ice better the spoon is less likely to be "fouled" by ice fragments sliding down the line and will continue to have good action even with a thin coat of ice on it.

Sweating Steelhead

Summer steelhead seem to tolerate fairly warm water temperatures but there is definitely a difference between just surviving and being willing to take a bait, lure or fly. In general these fish are quite active up to about 65 degrees and can still be caught fairly readily when the water is pushing 70. If my thermometer reads 72 I know that it is still possible to catch a summer run but I will usually try to search out cooler water. Frequently better conditions can be found where a colder tributary joins the main stream. Many times the steelhead will make a "temperature run" up the cooler tributary such as occurs in the rivers feeding the Columbia or the trout creeks emptying into the St. Joseph River.

My solution when water conditions are too warm is to search out cooler waters. The fish are more likely to be aggressive and even though there might be fewer of them the chances of hookups

A narrow chute on Oregon's Trask River.

are better. In addition steelhead caught in 70 degree water are sel-dom releasable. Usually you cannot even revive them and even if they do swim off they don't survive as evidenced by the mortalities that occurred in the St. Joesph River downstream from the Berrien Springs Dam before the ladders were finished. Here the fishing was hot (pun intended) because of a big concentration of fish and many fish were released because anglers quickly caught their limit. The district fisheries biologist documented that these released fish ended up dead downstream so the moral of the story is that if you plan on fishing for steelhead in warm water you better plan on keeping each one and quitting when you capture your limit.

In addition to finding cooler water through a different stream or location you can also concentrate your fishing during cooler times of the day. For the most part this is early morning as the water rarely cools fast enough to facilitate fishing in the evening.

11

Enhancing the Other Two-Thirds

I like to divide the sport of steelheading into three parts. The first is the preparation and anticipation of a fishing trip for the king of the river. The second is the actual fishing. And the third is the reminiscing and telling of fish stories to your steelheading buddies. Throughout the season the phone lines buzz with the network of steelie chasers making plans, checking on conditions, relating catches and losses, checking river levels, etc.

While many steelhead encounters leave strong impressions on our minds it is amazing how soon we forget the details of our outings on the river. Of course sometimes a hazy memory can be advantageous when it allows that big steelie to grow with time.

Spinner-caught hatchery steelhead with adipose fin clip.

You can enhance the memories of your fishing trips, better prepare yourself for future trips and improve your angling success by keeping a fishing log. This diary can range from a simple list of fish caught by date and body of water to a detailed recording of many of the factors that may affect the fish and the angler. You will want the log to provide all the information you need but not be a chore to fill out after your fishing trip.

Keeping fishing records can help your future angling success by helping to predict the timing of the runs. They will also make you more aware of how steelhead respond to different water levels, temperature, water clarity, etc. But, even if maintaining a log did nothing to improve my steelheading success I would still keep one. Why? Because reliving past outings and thinking about future trips (by looking through your log book) is a great way to spend a long winter evening.

Designing the Log Sheets

Since I spend almost all my fishing time wading streams for steelhead, salmon and resident trout I designed my record sheets for this type of fishing. The form is quite detailed but I don't always fill everything out completely. As an example let us go through the illustration of a recent Veteran's Day long weekend of steelheading with several regular fishing partners in northwestern lower Michigan.

The record form is designed so that it can be used for one or more fishing trips. The period covered is written in the upper left hand corner. It may be for a single outing, a week or month or a multiple day trip to the Oregon coast or northern Lake Michigan tributaries. Usually I try to save trees and stay on the same page until I run out of room for trips or, hopefully, fish entries.

For each day fished during the period I list the date in the upper left box. Information for the trip on that date is then carried across the top of the form.

On the example we see that the weather on the tenth of November was partly cloudy with an air temperature in the 50s. I did not note what the barometer was doing (P.C. = pressure change). Flint Watt and I stopped at the Sixth Street Dam on the Grand River to fish for a few hours on our way north to the Veteran's Day conclave. The water level was 5.80 at the gauge above the dam and the clarity was noted as slightly turbid. The water temperature was not taken and we fished from 2:30 to 5:30 in the afternoon. The next day I fished all day on the Little Manistee River starting below Six Mile Bridge and passing the bridge at 12:30. On the following day I tried the lower Betsie where we have the stretches numbered for reference. It was back on the Little Manistee for the fourth day of the trip and the upper Betsie was fished on the last day.

The Catch

The main body of the record sheet is for information about the fish caught. The date is filled in and then the fish that were caught on that day are listed. First, information about the fish, then equipment used and finally data on the stream are recorded.

As an example let's check out the only steelhead caught in the Grand on the tenth. It was a 30 inch male steelie that weighed ten and a half pounds. A number four silver French bladed spinner seduced the buck into hitting. Note: chemical symbols are used for the blade finish, for example Ag for silver and Au for gold (brass).

The line was 35 pound Spiderwire spooled on a Cardinal 6X spinning reel. The rod was homemade from Loomis popping rod 904 regular graphite blank. The retrieve was across and cover was provided by the Bridge Street abutment. The bottom was mostly bed rock, the depth was between five and six feet and the current speed was medium to fast.

Seven lake trout were also landed and released with an average weight of approximately eight pounds. Usually I list other anadromous species individually but here I got lazy with a bunch of lakers being caught in a relatively short amount of time.

As I switched to smaller rivers you can see that I changed gear. A seven foot rod was used with a Cardinal 4 and 14 pound test Trimax line. In addition to the usual French bladed spinners I fished with some in-line (IL) models. Also in the cover column if the spot is named we insert that (eg. "Bill's Landing") or sometimes the location is given, such as first highbank on the right rather than the specific cover.

In addition to recording my catch I also keep track of my partners' success. In this way when I compare time of year, stream and weather conditions and other factors to the catch it will not be biased if I had a particularly good or bad day.

Day	Weather	Temp.	B.P.	Stream	Location	Water Conditions In	Out
10	P.C	50's		Grand	64th St.	5.80 S.Turbid	same
11	P.C.→cldy			L.Manistee	6mi↓↑	2.0 Clear	
12	Clear			Betsie	6	Clear	
13	Drizzle		29.66	L.Manistee	6mid↑	2.0 Slight Stain	
14	Cldy	40's		Betsie	Psvtkn↑	Clear	

Day	Species	Sex	Lg.	Wt.	Lure	Line	Rod	Reel	Cast	Cover
10	Steelie	M	30	10½	4 Ag	35 SW	P904	C-6X	Across	Bridge W. Nbt.
"	Lnkers			7-?:8	"	"	"	"	"	
11	Steelie	M	29	9	4 Ag	14 TM	SM84H	C-4	Across	1st HB on right
"	"	F	34	11½	3 Ag	"	"	"	"	Bush
"	"	M	19	3	3 Av	"	"	"	"	Logs
"	"	M	29	9½	"	"	"	"	"	P.Line cdrf
"	"	F	27	8	4 JL Ag	"	"	"	"	Log
12	Steelie	M	18½	2½	3 Ag	14 TM	SMPMH	C-4	D+A	Logs
"	Brown	M	24	5½	"	"	"	"	Across	"
13	Steelie	F	31	11½	4 Ag	14 TM	SM84H	C-4	Across	1st HB right
"	"	M	33½	15½	"	"	"	"	Down	Deep pool
"	"	M	16	2	3 Ag	"	"	"	Across	Brush
"	"	F	22	4½	"	"	"	"	"	Bush
14	Steelie	F	31	10½	4 JL-Ag	14 Tm	SM84H	C-4	Across	Logs
"	"	F	30	9½	"	"	"	"	"	"
"	"	F	29	9	"	"	"	"	"	"
"	"	F	28	8	"	"	"	"	"	"
"	"	F	29	9	"	"	"	"	"	"
"	"	F	31	11	4 Ag	"	"	"	"	"
"	"	M	31½	11½	3 Ag	"	"	"	"	"
"	"	F	30	9½	4JL-Ag	"	"	"	"	"
"	"	F	32	12½	"	"	"	"	"	Bills Landing

Partner	Day	Location	Catch
F. Watt	10	Same	2 Steelhead 4 lnkers
"	11	L.M. 6n.↑↑	2 "
F. Eyer	11	Bear Cr.	3 "
K. Burka	11	L.M. 9mi.↑	3 "
F.E.+K.B.	12	Big Manistee	0 "
F. Watt	12	Lower Betsie, Upm B	0, 4 Steelhead
" "	13	Betsie-Upper	4 Steelhead
F. Eyer	13	" "	5 "
K. Burka	13	L. Manistee	2 "
"	14	Upper Betsie	3 "
F. Eyer	14	" "	2 "
F. Watt	14	" "	4 "

The success or failure of your partner can also help guide you where to fish next. For example Flint got fed up with the poor action in the lower Betsie on the 12th and drove to the upper part of the river where he caught four steelies in relatively short order. So Ken and Fred fished there with good success the next day and we all finished the trip on the upper Betsie where we had our best combined

Water Temperature		Time		Total Hours	Miscellaneous
In	Out	In	Out		
		2:30	5:30	3	
39		7:30-was-5:30		9	
40		8:00→4:30		8½	
		8:00-1-4:45		8¾	Passed 14 Anglers
42		8:00	3:00	7	

Bottom	Current	Depth	Kept?	Fin Clip	Time	Stomach Cont.
Rock	M-F	5-6'	N	None	5:00	
"	M	"	N			
S&G	S-M	4-5'	N	None	8:15	
"	"	"	N	"	11:15	
"	"	"	N	"	12:55	
"	M-F	"	N	"	2:30	
"	M	"	N	"	4:30	
Sand	S	5-6'	N	None	2:40	
"	S	"	N	"	4:35	
S&G	S-M	4-5'	N	None	9:05	
"	S	5-6'	N	"	10:00	
"	S-M	4-5'	N	"	11:05	
"	M	3-4'	N	"	4:40	
S&G	S-M	4-6'	N	None	8:30	
"	"	"	N	Ad	8:35	
"	"	"	N	None	8:45	
"	"	"	N	"	8:55	
"	"	"	N	"	10:30	
"	"	"	N	"	11:45	
"	"	4'	N	"	12:05	
"	M	3-4'	N	Dorsal	2:35	
"	"	4-5'	N	None	2:50	

Lures Lost	Fish Lost	How	Other encounters
10th - 1	10th - zero steelies		
11th - 3	11th - 1 steelie - Hook pulled	~ 4F + 1 FTH	
12th - 1	12th - 0		3 FTH - unknown species
13th - 2	13th - 1 steelie H#0		2 FTH + 1 F
14th - 1	14th 0		1 FTH

day of the whole outing even though we quit early to head home.

Telling Stories

Having a record of your partners' catch also helps when the

gang gets together and recounts those fishing trips. These Veteran's Day excursions have special meaning to Fred Eyer and me as the example log sheet documents the 26th consecutive November 11th that we have fished together. A pretty remarkable record considering we both were involved in raising families during this time and no domestic obligation or family illness interfered with our annual November rendevous on the river. Fred is also an avid fishing log keeper and you better have an escape route planned if you get caught in a room when we're reminiscing about past outings.

Just for the heck of it I also note how many lures I lose. This gives me an idea about how snaggy and deep a section of river is but mainly I just like to see how many of my 30 cent homemade spinners I go through in a season. As you can see the snags were not too tough on me over this long weekend.

Keeping track of lost fish will tell me if they were hitting and I was losing them or they were just plain not there or turned off. I also keep track of other encounters in this column such as follows (F) and missed strikes (FTH=failed to hook).

Keep it Simple

Now you could also include solunar table data, overall angling pressure, moon phase and many other factors. But for most people a much simpler form would do just fine.

I suggest that you start out with just a list of the fish caught along with the date and location. You could put some details down about individual steelhead while just noting total numbers of stream trout or other smaller fish.

At the end of the year or season you can compile a summary of your catch. This will let you compare average sizes between rivers and years. If you keep track of time spent you can make interesting comparisons on your catch per hour or day on the river. I place my summary sheet in my log book as a divider between seasons.

There is a drawback to keeping fishing records. It makes it more difficult to make that monster steelhead grow with time. When that fishing buddy or grandchild gets a chance to peruse your log book it may be hard to explain why that 19 pound steelhead you caught in your favorite river ten years ago is only listed at 16 and a 1/2 pounds in the diary.

While your log will help you pick the best days to go fishing don't let this new knowledge inhibit you from going steelheading when conditions don't seem to be prime. There will always be exceptions. For example the very low and falling barometer on the 13th should have turned off the steelies but all four of us had good success and I caught my largest steelhead of the trip. Of course, when you have an either/or choice on fishing days your log will help you pick the day most likely to be productive.

12

Steelheading **T**ips

Here are some additional ideas and suggestions on improving your success and increasing your enjoyment of the great sport of steelhead fishing.

Rising Water Temperature

Steelhead can detect very slight changes in water temperature and they are more active when the temperature is rising. This is especially true in the winter so on cold days concentrate your fishing from mid-morning to late afternoon when the air temperature is warming. Remember that the water temperature can rise with rising air temperature or sunshine even when the air is much colder than the water.

Anticipate Strikes

Keep a positive attitude and be alert at all times when fishing for steelhead, imagining that a big silver fish is going to grab your offering the next moment. It is difficult to maintain this level of concentration all day but the take of a steelie can be very subtle or very quick and the hook needs to be driven home immediately.

Snagged Lures

When your lure is hung up across or downstream let the current help free it. Release several yards of line into the flow and then sharply raise your rod. The resistance of the line in the current will pull at the lure from a different angle and often release the hook from the bottom.

Manageable Mono

To make monofilament line more manageable, especially

freshly spooled new line, soak your spool in a dish of water for a few minutes before fishing. If you forget you can always dunk the spool in the river for a minute or two.

Breaking Off

If you are unable to free a snagged lure or drift rig do not break the line against your rod. Friction on the guides will often cause the line to break in the rod leaving a long length of line in the water. Instead, point your rod at the snag and slowly pull until something gives. Using a lighter leader will also prevent line loss but even the heavier mainline mono will frequently break at the rod tip if you repeatedly jerk hard with the rod against the snag. If the line does break in the rod or your hand, tie on another lure and try to cast over and catch the trailing line in the river. Bring the line up to you and try to break it again at the knot. You may even get your rig back on the second try.

Tight Drag

Keep your drag set near the breaking strength of your line to maximize your hook setting power. If you can hear the drag slip when you set the hook into a snag or fish it is set too light. After the fish is hooked you can lighten up the drag a bit for the battle.

Casting Plugs

Diving plugs are great lures for steelhead and they are not limited to drop back or back trolling methods. Try casting deep diving plugs quartering downstream and reel just enough to get them to dive near the bottom and sweep across the current.

Ice in the Guides

Removing ice in guides is a constant chore for midwestern winter river anglers. Remember that as long as the river is above freezing all you have to do is dip the rod in the current to remove the ice. This works even when the water is only 33 degrees but obviously takes longer the closer it is to freezing. When the water thermometer registers 32 you will have to warm the guides by hand or mouth and then pop the ice out with your thumb.

Polishing Lures

You can increase your chances of getting a steelhead to notice and strike your lure by making sure it is bright and highly visible.

Dark male steelhead caught with a bright spinner.

For brass, nickel, copper and chrome lures use a quality metal polish. For genuine silver plated lures use a baking soda and water paste or a gentle silver polish to prevent removal of the silver plate. If you are unable to remove tarnish on the spinner blade or spoon try covering the areas with fluorescent or prism lure tape.

Drying Lures

The blades of shiny spinners and spoons should be carefully wiped dry before they are returned to your lure box. This will prevent water spotting and tarnishing copper, silver and brass finishes. Use a soft cloth or paper towel to wipe them down. Also when you are done fishing opening lure boxes to the air will allow any residual moisture to escape and prevent the hooks from rusting.

Preventing Broken Rods

Graphite ferruled rods are often broken unnecessarily. The breakage is not due to abuse by the angler, car doors or faulty construction. Improper seating of the ferrule is the culprit. It is very important that you join the sections of your rod together very snugly. Any play in the connection puts extra stress in the ferrule area and may result in a sickening crack when you set the hook. A teflon type lubricant facilitates the firm seating of the ferrule without sticking.

Check Guides

Examine your rod guides for grooves and rough spots which can rapidly wear your line. Nylon stocking material or cotton swabs pulled through the guides will help identify any damaged areas. Even though ceramic and silicon carbide guides will not groove they can fracture and the hard sharp edges will quickly damage your line.

Sunlight Damage

Direct sunshine has a detrimental effect on many items of steelhead tackle. Avoid storing your equipment in cars, boats or near windows where it will be exposed to sunlight. The sun's rays are especially harmful to waders, raincoats, monofilament line, rod finishes and plastic lures.

Tuning Spinners

Many of you are familiar with the need to tune plugs so they will run true but tuning spinners can also be important to success. If your spinner is not revolving easily, check to see if the shaft is straight and the top tie on loop is in direct line with the shaft. An offset loop will cause you to pull the spinner at an angle and require a faster retrieve to make it spin. Make sure the clevis is not bent and there is no corrosion on the shaft.

Change Line Often

The most important link between you and that trophy steelhead, your line, is also the least expensive. Stretching, wetting and drying, and abrasions all slowly weaken your monofilament. Changing your line is good insurance against a disappointing break off. When replacing your line discard (recycle) only the top fifty yards or so. Attach the fresh line with a blood knot and refill the spool. Since you seldom use the line deep in the spool it is not necessary to completely refill the spool.

Twisted Line

If your line becomes twisted when you are steelheading simply cut off your terminal rig or lure and feed the line into the river. Pump it a few times and then reel it back in, applying tension from your fingers. Repeat if needed.

Something Different

If the steelhead are ignoring your offering try changing to something different. Size, color and type of lure can all be varied. If a large silver spoon is not working switch to a smaller brass spinner.

When eggs aren't attracting the silver migrant's attention try a bright colored yarn ball or drift bobber. Or, perhaps just adding a piece of yarn or a drift bobber to your egg cluster will do the trick.

Odor Free

While steelhead are primarily sight feeders they have a very sensitive olfactory system. Scent plays a big role in steelhead finding their natal streams and they are very sensitive to negative odors such as those from human hands. Many products are sold as fish attractants and human odor masks. Since steelhead are not actively feeding it is more important to remove the negative odors than to make the lure smell like food. Wash your lures and hands with a soap designed for this purpose and minimize subsequent handling of your terminal tackle.

Replace File

A file works great to sharpen hook points but after lots of use it will start to dull. When this happens simply replace it with a new model. Files are inexpensive and the time saved in making your hook points sticky sharp far outweighs its cost. You can prolong the life of your file by making sure it does not rust. Allow it to dry after fishing and periodically spray it with a water displacing lubricant.

Single Eggs

A single egg is the most natural way to present spawn to steelhead and is especially effective when the water is low and ultra clear. Use fine wire hooks and toughen the skin of the eggs by partial drying, boiling or mixing with salt or borax. You want the egg to be tough enough to stay on the hook yet still be crushable when the steelie takes so that the "flavor" is released.

Fast Water Eggs

When fast, tumbling water makes it difficult to keep natural skein spawn or single eggs on the hook try using plastic eggs or yarn balls. Soak the imitations in the real thing or apply attractant scents so the fakes will smell and taste like natural spawn.

Floats and Wind

It is very difficult to detect strikes when drifting bait or flies on a windy day. This is especially true when fishing strong current a considerable distance away. Use a bobber to detect pickups under these conditions. If you use a float with an adjustable quill set it so most of it is under the water and out of the wind.

Removing Loops

Since a loop will be laid down on your spinning reel spool at the beginning of the retrieve and will probably not be noticed until your next casting attempt, you must be careful not to create a bigger tangle as you pull line off the spool to remove the loop. This is especially true when the loop is large and deeply buried. Each coil around the spool can end up wrapped around the loop as you pull it off. To avoid creating a big tangle, pull line off the spool, separating the loop from the line after every two or three pulls.

Last Cast

Experience is still the best teacher and that is especially true relative to steelhead fishing. Hopefully the information in this volume will help you add to and hone your skills more quickly. And, perhaps give you some new ideas to try on your next river outing.

Spend every minute on the river that you can and fill your senses with the world of the steelhead. Please revere this great game fish and release most of what you catch, especially the wild fish. They are the future of our special sport.

About The Author

Jim Bedford is an extremely avid river fisherman who spends 500 hours a year trying to catch the king of the river, the steelhead. He has successfully fished for steelhead in Alaska, British Columbia, Washington, Oregon, and Indiana as well as his home state of Michigan. Jim has been writing about steelhead in regional and national magazines since 1974 and has been teaching community college angling classes for the last 15 years. He has graduate degrees in fisheries biology and aquatic entomology and pays the bills by working as an environmental toxicologist for the State of Michigan. Every now and then the waders are given a chance to dry and the tennis court, garden, or bridge table is allowed some token time.